C000103497

FASTER THAN SOUND

FASTER THAN SOUND

Harvey Shapiro

SOUTH BRUNSWICK AND NEW YORK: A. S. BARNES AND COMPANY
LONDON: THOMAS YOSELOFF LTD

© 1975 by A. S. Barnes and Co.

A. S. Barnes and Co., Inc.
Cranbury, New Jersey 08512

Thomas Yoseloff Ltd
108 New Bond Street
London W1Y OQX, England

Library of Congress Cataloging in Publication Data

Shapiro, Harvey, 1937-
    Faster than sound.

    Bibliography: p.
    Includes index.
    1. Automobile racing—History. 2. Automobiles,
Racing—Speed records. 3. Automobile racing—Biography.
I. Title.
GV1029.15.S38   796.7'2   73-22610
ISBN 0-498-01507-6

PRINTED IN THE UNITED STATES OF AMERICA

This book is humbly dedicated to those gutsy drivers—past, present, and future—who put aside their human fears in pursuit of the elusive world land-speed record. I have known, admired and even envied them.

Contents

Foreword

"Records are made to be broken. I don't plan on holding the record forever, but I'd like to be the first to go through the sound barrier. It's a great challenge to do something nobody else has done. I'd like to be able to say we did it...put together a team, built a car and drove it faster than sound"—GARY GABELICH.

"How many people really enjoy what they're doing? I think I'm one of the lucky ones. I'm completely satisfied with my life. It's gotta be good when you can make a living at your hobby as many years as I have"—ART ARFONS.

Acknowledgments

Books aren't written overnight. This one was the product of 10 years of research. My humble thanks to the many people who have helped along the way: Gary Gabelich; Art Arfons; Craig Breedlove; Bobby Summers; Mickey Thompson; Walt Arfons; Bob Tatroe; Dr. Nathan Ostich; Bill Frederick; Vladimir K. Nikitin, Soviet Institute for Automobiles and Roads, Kharkov, USSR; Clyde Hayes, NASA Langley Research Center, Hampton, Virginia; Bradford A. Evans, NASA, Ames Research Center, Moffett Field, California; John Swihart, Boeing; H.K. Gagos, McDonnell-Douglas Aircraft; Alan Pope, Sandia Laboratories, Albuquerque, New Mexico; Kenneth Norris, Norris Brothers, Ltd., England; Richard Keller, Pete Farnsworth, Ray Dausman, Reaction Dynamics, Milwaukee, Wisconsin; Deke Houlgate; Allen Wolfe; Collene Campbell; Clayton Gontner; Firestone Tire & Rubber Company; Goodyear Tire and Rubber Company; Ford Motor Company; Chrysler Motor Company; American Gas Association.

Institute of Gas Technology; Cornell Aeronautical Laboratory, Buffalo, New York; United States Auto Club; Dunlop Tire and Rubber Company; Wynn Oil Company; Holloman Air Force Base, Almogordo, New Mexico; The Associated Press; *Deseret News,* Salt Lake City, Utah; *Salt Lake Tribune; Akron Beacon Journal*, Akron, Ohio; Australian Information Service; Australian Consulate General, New York; News Limited, Sydney, Australia; *The Advertiser*, Adelaide, Australia; *Los Angeles Times; Los Angeles Herald-Examiner*.

Museum of Speed, Daytona Beach, Florida; Birthplace of Speed Association, Daytona Beach, Florida; *Hot Rod Magazine; Mechanix Illustrated; Sports Illustrated; Long Beach Press-Telegram*, Long Beach, California; *Popular Mechanics; Time; Motor Trend*.

Daily Sketch, London, England; *Daily Mail*, London, England; *Daily Mirror*, London, England; *The Evening News,* London, England; *The Daily Telegraph*, London, England.

FASTER THAN SOUND

1

The Sound Barrier—Myth or Mankiller?

In December of 1903, two bicycle shop owners shattered an age-old "barrier" that man had once considered impenetrable. Although their historic flight lasted only 12 seconds and covered 500 feet, Orville and Wilbur Wright proved that man could fly. Today, supersonic aircraft streak across the sky at speeds surpassing 2,000 miles per hour.

In 1926, rocketry pioneer Robert Goddard launched his homemade liquid propellant missile. The rocket "soared" to the height of 220 feet in two-and-one-half seconds. Today, massive Saturn rockets carry man into outer space.

Man, the great innovator, has applied the science of aerodynamics with the thrust of the jet and rocket engine to race across the surface of the land at speeds that only an electronic timer can record.

He has traveled through the measured mile in less than six seconds...at a speed of 622.407. But he wants to go even faster.

Tick...tick...tick...tick. Just four seconds in time. It doesn't seem like much. But to a man riding a fiery chariot it could be a blast-off into history or a one-way ticket to the grave.

Man is now taking dead aim on the biggest speed prize of all...The Sound Barrier. It is estimated a car must travel 720 to 750 miles per hour to crack the mysterious barrier.

Laboratory tests conducted in sophisticated wind tunnels indicate a land-bound car can safely exceed the speed of sound without disintegrating under the killer force of unseen shock waves, or become a wingless plane.

But no one really knows for sure what will happen during this assault into the unknown. That doesn't mean, however, that no one is willing to find out. On the contrary.

As many as seven different contenders flying the proud colors of three countries could be involved in "The Great Race." For the first time since land speed racing came into being in 1898, the Soviet Union has entered the chase.

Five cars with supersonic capability could represent the United States, while Australian industry is backing the exotic rocket racer, "Courage of Australia".

Reigning land speed king Gary Gabelich of Long Beach, California, and five-time record holder Craig Breedlove, of Spirit of America fame, talk of a full-blast drag race at the Bonneville Salt Flats in Utah.

Art Arfons, who battled Breedlove through two stormy years (1964-1965) and set three land speed records in the span, plans his assault in a 17,500-horsepower jet, Green Monster.

"Pollution Packer", a rocket-powered dragster owned by Minnesota industrialist Tony Fox, has been clocked at 322 miles an hour for the quarter-mile. The king-size version, "Proud American", could reach speeds of 1,000 miles an hour.

Art's older brother Walt, who introduced the rocket age to land speed racing, envisions another rocket car or a steam-driven racer. A prototype steam-powered dragster has already demonstrated tremendous speed potential.

The Soviet Institute for Automobiles and Roads in Kharkov has announced plans to build a car capable of crashing the sound barrier. Vladimir K. Nikitin, chief engineer and designer, said: "I have no doubt that it will be the fastest in the world. We propose to overcome the sound barrier with it. The first testing field will probably be the frozen

The early stages of The Fox Group's "Pollution Packer."
Courtesy The Fox Group.

surface of a lake." The 30-foot long car, powered by multiple gas-turbine engines, has been named "Hadi-9". It is the latest in a series of high-speed cars built by the Institute.

"Hadi is a word composed of the first four letters of the name of our institute—Harkov Automobile-Road Institute," Nikitin explained.

"Some of our automobiles—Hadi-5, Hadi-7, Hadi-8—have set all-Union or international records of speed. It's but natural that we want to construct a new car to try the luck and compete for the absolute world record.

"Who will drive the car? Well, it will make the first steps with me, under my direction. We are planning to test it on Baskunchak Lake."

Because of the risk involved, the first tests

through the sound barrier will be made using radio signals rather than a human being, said the Soviet designer-driver.

On October 23, 1970, Gary Gabelich set a new two-way record of 622.407 MPH in the rocket-powered "Blue Flame." Using 13,000 of the car's potential 22,000 pounds of thrust, the 31-year-old Californian made back-to-back runs of 617 and 627 miles an hour. His peak speed through the measured mile was 640 to 660.

"The car felt very well at 650. You didn't have to drive it...you just aimed it. I had to do very minor compensating to get the car through the measured mile. It handled like a car going 75 or 80 on the freeway."

Gabelich had hoped to attack the sound barrier

in "Blue Flame", but his plans were changed when the sponsoring natural gas industry decided to retire the car.

"It just takes money to crack the barrier and they feel they're proven their point. Instead of spending up to $1 million to go faster, they want to put it into research.

"I think "Blue Flame" is very well designed and very well built. With 22,000 pounds of thrust—58,000 horsepower—I think it could run 800 to 850 safely."

A driver without a car, Gabelich began the tedious task of finding sponsorship for his own rocket racer.

"I can build a car to break the sound barrier for $500,000. We've got the team together that can do the job, including people who worked on "Blue Flame". My car will be longer, lighter, have less frontal area and boast more power. I want to be the first to break the barrier...then the first to go 1,000 miles an hour on land."

Barrels of hydrogen peroxide, tanks of nitrogen are readied to transfer into the 16 gal. tank of the "Pollution Packer." *Courtesy The Fox Group.*

What will it take to do the job?

"Instead of 13,000 pounds of thrust where we went over 650, we'll have 40,000 pounds or well over 100,000 horsepower. You just put it to the wood and use all of it. You have to determine how much, how far and how long you're gonna run.

"It has a throttable rocket engine, but what I'd like to do is get back from the measured mile and drive it the same each time. If it takes one-quarter mile to enter the mile at 700 and peak out at 800, that's fine. If it takes a mile to get that fast, that's fine too.

"I want to make a giant drag race out of it. I want to accelerate as quick as I can, as hard as I can for a short distance. I'd like to race Breedlove. I think running both cars at the same time for the sound barrier would add a lot to the show."

Gabelich will increase his speed by increments of 100 miles an hour until the rocket racer reaches about 650 miles per hour.

"From that point we'll go for the sound barrier in a two-out-of-three match race." His car will be propelled by hydrogen peroxide, or by a mixture of peroxide and liquified natural gas (LNG).

Breedlove's 44-foot long "Spirit of America-Sonic II will develop 35,000 pounds of rocket thrust, burning a fuel misture of unsymmetrical dimenthyl hydrazene and nitrogen tetra-oxide.

While the five-time land speed king doesn't like to talk about "the numbers," or maximum speed he anticipates reaching in the "Spirit," "it will be extremely fast. It will be capable of doing zero to 974 miles an hour in 24 seconds. I'm not saying whether of not it gets turned on that fast, but that is the potential.

"It's very easy to talk about speeds like that, but they are very hard to come by. However, when I calculated the speed I was very conservative in the estimate."

The cars will run parallel, about 150 yards apart. The winner is expected to pocket $500,000 in the greatest race of the century. The money will be raised through sale of movie and television rights.

If that wasn't enough incentive, Breedlove is still steaming over inferences that he had been considered as a driver for "Blue Flame" but was rejected in favor of Gabelich.

"I didn't like the way they implied I was getting too old. Gary's a great guy and an extremely competent driver, but they made some statements about me that I didn't particularly care for.

"The truth is that I considered the car and turned the ride down for two reasons. First, the financial arrangements were not satisfactory. But

"Pollution Packer" at the line for Memorial Day drag racing
at Union Grove, Wisconsin. *Courtesy The Fox Group.*

Fox's "Sonic Challenger" snowmobile, powered by a
2,500-lb. thrust hydrogen peroxide rocket. *Courtesy The Fox
Group.*

second and most important, I wanted to have some sort of control over design. I particularly didn't like the idea of sitting between the fuel tank and the motor.

"Rocket engines need development. History records that they are unstable until they are fully developed. The engine they used is nowhere as stable as the engine I have. TRW has spent $92 million making mine safe and reliable.

"During that period the X-15 had the back of it blown off in flight, and that's not a couple of guys in a garage building the X-15, that's North American Rockwell."

TRW is Thompson Ramo Woolridge, an Ohio company formed by a merger of Thompson Products, a Cleveland firm that makes auto parts, and Ramo Woolridge, a space-age think tank company.

Simon Ramo and Dean Woolridge are regarded as two of the United States' leading experts in space exploration. TRW developed many of the products that went into the moon shots.

An autopilot system will be incorporated into Breedlove's car. "It's a system to compensate and change the lift of the car as it goes through the transsonic speed range," he explains.

"It monitors the loading from the front wheel and adjusts the canard fins accordingly. In other words, what we're trying to do is maintain a static loading for the entire run."

Gary Gabelich, however, would rather drive the car himself.

"They have devices that can measure things and make responses faster than humans, they say. But I think it takes a lot out of it. I'd rather have it manually controlled. You don't really have to do that much controlling if the car is designed right.

"Our car is designed with one degree downtilt. It's flat on the top and has an arch on the bottom and there are other design things that should make it go very straight."

While Gabelich and Breedlove exchange barbs, Art Arfons looks forward to his first Bonneville appearance since 1966. Seeking to regain his land speed title, Arfons crashed his jet-powered "Green Monster" at an estimated 620 miles per hour.

Miraculously, he suffered only cuts, abrasions and salt burns. Out of the ashes of his car, he built a faster and more streamlined "Monster."

The "Green Monster" is 22 feet long, 76 inches wide, 38 inches high and weighs 5,810 pounds— 2,600 pounds less than its famed predecessor.

Campaigning the 17,500-horsepower jet on the drag strips for several years, Arfons hit a peak speed of 273.55 for the quarter. "It will go from

Dave Anderson (left) and Tony Fox, with "Pollution Packer." *Courtesy The Fox Group.*

zero to 650 in 14 seconds," he points out. He may make his assault on solid wheels— something that has not been attempted before.

"Experts at Firestone tell me there wouldn't be enough traction for steering with the solid wheels. I believe there will be, so we'll find out when we get back to the Flats. There's no way to test out my theory, other than to actually run on the salt."

While Arfons boasts the smallest package of dynamite, "Courage of Australia" at 60 feet in length, rates as the longest car in land speed history.

Built by Bill Frederick of Chatsworth, California, the $250,000 racer is designed to hit 1,000 miles per hour in 27½ seconds, burning hydrogen peroxide.

It should reach 300 in three seconds, 600 in 12½ seconds and the sound barrier in 18 seconds—that's 759 at Lake Eyre in Australia.

Because of the car's tremendous speed potential, it is estimated that driver Vic Wilson, an Australian, will require only a maximum of six miles.

How do you stop a 64,000-horsepower car?

Braking of the "Courage" consists of a double backup chute system.

At speeds between 400 to 700 miles per hour, a small 8-foot drogue chute is employed. When speeds are reduced to 150-300, a 16-foot ribbon-type drag chute is deployed for the rest of the braking process. Rear disc brakes assist the drag chute in bringing the three-wheeler to a stop.

To prepare for the sound barrier, Frederick built a 27-foot prototype rocket dragster—"Courage of Australia I." On November 11, 1971, the Wynn's-sponsored car turned in a spectacular 311.41 run in just 5.107 seconds at Orange County International Raceway in Irvine, California.

"I really enjoyed the ride," said Vic Wilson," and I didn't believe the car had gone that fast. "Courage" used 75 percent of its 12,000 horsepower.

"It was a really smooth ride," said the

The "Pollution Packer" at Bonneville. *Courtesy The Fox Group.*

Anderson pops the chute as another record run is made on the salt flats. *Courtesy The Fox Group.*

28-year-old driver. "Sometimes when I go fast my eyeballs vibrate, but not this time."

He can't wait to drive the sound barrier car.

"Our calculations are that its potential speed is 1,000 miles per hour, but we will be aiming for about 680 on our shakedown runs."

When completed, "Proud American" will be 45 feet in length, 24 inches wide and 34 inches high.

The driver will sit in the tail section. A hydrogen peroxide rocket will power the car, generating a thrust of 35,000 pounds.

Its prototype, "Pollution Packer," was the first rocket dragster to run under National Hot Rod Association (NHRA) sanction. During a two-day period — September 30-October 1, 1972 — drivers Dave Anderson and Paula Murphy combined to set 13 national and international speed acceleration records in rocket, unlimited and category "C" classes at the Bonneville Salt Flats.

The record of 234,775 established by Anderson in the kilometer required a terminal velocity of nearly 479 miles an hour.

During the 1973 NHRA Spring Nationals at Columbus, Ohio, Anderson turned in a blistering 322 MPH performance for the quarter mile. His elapsed time was 4.99 seconds. "It was just a smooth, straight ride," he said.

Anderson, however, will not drive the supersonic car. He was killed in a drag race accident on March 30, 1974 at Charlotte, N.C., when the parachute of his rocket-powered racer failed to open. He was traveling 250 miles an hour at the time.

Two teammates were also killed when Anderson hit the brakes, spinning "Pollution Packer" into their path.

Although semi-retired from the speed game, Walt Arfons would like nothing better than to close out his notable career in a puff of steam.

As far back as 1966, Arfons experimented with a steam-driven dragster. In its maiden run, driver Bobby Tatroe flipped at 200 miles an hour, rolling six times before the car finally came to rest.

"Man I'm telling you...that baby was something. I never felt anything like this in my life for get-up-and-go," said the man who made land speed racing history the previous year by driving the first rocket-powered racer.

All it would take to get the massive "Wingfoot Express" ready for the sound barrier are some minor modifications.

"Seven thousand pounds of the "Wingfoot's" 10,000-pound starting weight would be its 'fuel' load of steam," claims Arfons. "And that whole 7,000 pounds of steam will be released in the first 30 or 40 seconds of the run."

A hydraulically operated throttle valve would be the engine's only moving part. "Basically, the rocket system would consist of a tank, heating unit and throttle."

Arfons plans to fit the fiberglass nose of the "Wingfoot" to an exceptionally durable, highly polished stainless steel tank 30 inches in diameter.

Land speed record rules call for two runs through the measured mile within 60 minutes. "By having a tank ready with water preheated to 470 degrees Fahrenheit, we can shave turn-around time to under 20 minutes."

Is the sound barrier myth or mankiller?

On October 14, 1947, U.S. Air Force Captain Charles B. Yeager established aviation history by piloting his rocket-powered Bell X-1 through the sound barrier.

Dropped from the belly of a B-29 bomber at an altitude of 35,000 feet, Yeager relied on his four rocket engines developing 6,000 pounds of thrust to push X-1 to a speed of 1,200 miles per hour.

Now supersonic planes travel at more than three times the speed of sound.

On March 19, 1954, Air Force Colonel John Paul Stapp, a veteran of aviation medical research, rode a rocket sled to a record 632 miles per hour.

The 2,000-pound sled, propelled by nine rockets unleashing 40,000 pounds of thrust, required just five seconds on its run down the 3,500-foot track at Holloman Air Force Base in Alamogoro, New Mexico.

Three years later, a driverless sled hit 2,075 over a two-rail track. A monorail vehicle has reached 2,850 miles per hour.

But can a race car hold the ground at supersonic speed? Land speed drivers and builders and top NASA and aircraft experts, as well as an automobile wind tunnell testing expert, have varied opinions.

First, the drivers:

"A lot of aerodynamists think the pressures will blow the car off the ground. Some think the pressure will crush the car. The sound barrier presents a whole set of problems," says Gabelich.

"When a plane breaks the sound barrier the shock wave is despersed through the air. We don't know what the shock wave will do. Conceivably, it could bounce off the ground and flip the car.

"It's a gamble, but I really believe we can break the sound barrier with no problems. I'm putting a lot of faith in the people I'm working with."

Breaking the barrier is only the beginning, according to the fastest man on wheels.

"The record will always climb. I don't think there's an ultimate speed limit, but there's probably an ultimate limit in the tires that are available now. Goodyear has a tire they say is good for 800. After that it may be possible that cars will have to be built with aluminum or magnesium wheels that are stressed very well with rubber bonded to them.

"Someday they'll be running on light rays, laser beams, or something like that. The amount of distance could have a lot to do with the ultimate speed limit. Under the right conditions at Bonneville, it's possible a car would run there anywhere from 800 to 1,000 miles an hour. Way out."

Craig Breedlove has a different opinion.

"Transsonic speed is the real problem, but I think the car can get through safely. A driver just can't charge at the sound barrier. It has to be approached gradually. When my front wheels went off the ground at 600 (in "Spirit of America-Sonic I"), it reaffirmed the belief that you have to go up in planned speed increments.

"If you increase speed 100 miles an hour at a crack, you run into behavorial patterns you weren't expecting. If you increase the speed in lesser increments, you can get a good idea each time of the problem you'll encounter at the next stage."

Breedlove belongs to a class of wind tunnel non-believers.

After the record run, Dave Anderson (left) and Tony Fox. *Courtesy The Fox Group.*

"Airplane designers aren't much help to a man building a land racer, because conditions on the ground aren't at all like five miles up.

"It's like comparing walking through air with walking through water. All wind-tunnel data is useless to us, and so is the performance of high-speed sleds. They're locked to their tracks."

"I think it's gonna be a hell of a job to go through the barrier," contends three-time land speed king Art Arfons. "Very few airplanes that the government has today are allowed to go through at that altitude—4,000 feet at Bonneville—because of the density of the air. Most can't go supersonic below 5,000 feet."

Arfons feels it will take brute force, rather than aerodynamic design, to get the job done at Bonneville.

"If you had 20 miles of salt, it would take less power and a good design, but with 10-11 miles of total running room, it will take nothing but power."

Although Arfons' "Green Monster" has a speed potential of 800, the Ohio driver first plans to reach 650.

"Although I'll use full power from the four-stage afterburner, I don't plan to keep full power for more than 18 seconds. That should be enough to reach 650.

"I could run on all four stages longer, but I'm not about to be a hero. I don't know what will happen to a car once it reaches supersonic speed...no one really does.

"All it will cost me is one car if it doesn't make it through the barrier. And I don't want to be in the cockpit to find out."

Once the "Green Monster" hits 650, Arfons plans to send his jet car through the sound barrier via remote control. If it passes the test, he'll take over.

And, like Breedlove, Arfons minimizes the value of wind tunnel testing for high-speed runs. "Donald Campbell's "Bluebird" was tunnel tested, yet it flew 800 feet in the air at about 350 miles an hour."

Although Bobby Summers, holder of the land speed mark for wheel-driven cars, has no intention of attacking the barrier, he thinks such a feat is possible.

"It will take quite a bit of aerodynamic development in building a car that is capable of going faster than sound. I don't think it would be wise to attempt it without good wind tunnel testing and a very competent aerodynamist.

"I think wind tunnel testing is very critical. It now only tells the speed potential of the car, but its directional stability as well."

"Once the sound barrier is broken," points out designer-builder Walt Arfons, "it will be the end of the land speed record attempts. From then on, it will only be a matter of going faster.

"How many persons know who followed Lindbergh across the Atlantic and Bannister under the four-minute mile?

"There will be a slight shudder as the car goes through the barrier, perhaps not enough to notice. If the car doesn't blast through, the shock waves will tear it apart."

Arfons maintains rocket power is far superior to jet-thrust at supersonic speed. "A rocket has no intake, so it can have a clean streamlined body to break air and shock waves. The steam-thrust car falls in the rocket category.

"A jet intake has to reach out ahead of the car to

suck air. This causes turbulence quite ahead of the car and more turbulence as the air goes into the intake. When the jet is shut off, the air in front packs.

"Before, the car was cutting a hole through the wall of air. Suddenly, there's no hole. The rear of the car would go all over.

"With a rocket, the resistance is behind instead of ahead. This keeps the car straight, on the same principle as a flying arrow. The car slips through cleanly.

"We proved this in 1965 with the "Wingfoot Express," for which I used solid fuel JATO rockets. The "Wingfoot" reached 580 in 15 seconds and the fuel ran out. We'd have been okay if the rockets had held a sustained speed.

"There were no handling problems. The driver (Bob Tatroe) didn't have to move the steering wheel."

When Gary Gabelich set the land speed record of 622 in 1970, the tops of the huge rear wheels on his rocket-powered "Blue Flame" were traveling at supersonic speeds. Sonic booms exploded rapid-fire, punching holes three inches deep and four feet in diameter behind the wheels. Bill Frederick was a member of the "Blue Flame" team, helping to build the car's rocket.

"It was frightening. No car had ever traveled that fast so we didn't know what to expect. I think we've got the problem beat, but we won't really know until Vic (Wilson) takes the car through the sound barrier. Until that happens, we're only theorizing."

Harold Turner, director of the China Lake Research Center, a U.S. Naval Ordinance test station in California, has acted as consultant on the "Courage II" project.

Turner indicated that "Courage" will experience a large drag rise in the transonic area and the close ground proximity would cause the three-wheeler to experience violent shock waves that reflect between the ground and the under side of the body.

This fact demanded that the car's cross-sectional configuration be triangular in shape, with the apex at the underside to the body to alleviate any sudden pitching moment oscillations generated by these shock waves or pressure build-ups.

Testing also indicated "Courage" must have a dropped nose cone and a slight negative angle of attack to yield to the smallest pressure drag and zero lift.

Rear wheels extend beyond the aft end of the body (to comply with the "aerodynamic area rule") and have a wide track to ensure roll stability. A vertical stabilizing fin provides yaw stability.

None of the drivers consider their task lightly. Pushing the land speed record from 394 to 622 miles an hour in eight years (1963-1970) was relatively simple.

Just consider the switch from piston power to the thrust of a jet or rocket engine, from the 2,500 horsepower of John Cobb's ancient "Railton Special," to the potential 22,000 horsepower of Gary Gabelich's rocket-propelled "Blue Flame."

But pushing the mark to 750 miles an hour...through the sound barrier... is another matter.

Only when man takes a dead aim at the barrier will the million dollar question be answered: Myth or mankiller?

2
The Experts Speak—Do They Agree?

"Theoretically, there is no reason why a land-bound vehicle could not be made to travel faster than sound."

"The entire project represents a rather dangerous undertaking."

"I would be more concerned about keeping my tires together than I would be about the integrity of the car and the engine."

"Wind tunnel tests would be mandatory to the design of a successful land speed car."

The opinions vary. Even the experts who should know aren't in full agreement whether a land-bound car can crash the sound barrier.

To understand the problem, a study of sound itself is required.

Although invisible, the air is composed of countless numbers of extremely tiny atoms and molecules of nitrogen, oxygen and other gases. Each atom or molecule is so tiny that some 400 billion of them can be found in every cubic inch of the air at sea level.

In constant motion, they travel in all directions, bumping into each other, and striking any object they encounter. In doing so, they exert pressure. When waves of varying air pressure strike our ears, we "hear" them as sounds.

Sound waves can be likened to the ripples created by the dropping of a stone into a body of still water. Traveling outward, the sound waves eventually pulsate against the ears, much as water pulsates when agitated.

The speed of sound is the time it takes for sound to travel from its source to the receiver, which, in turn, depends upon the speed at which the gas molecules "carrying" the pressure waves are moving.

Generally speaking, sound travels at 1000 feet per second; but varies with altitude, air density and temperature. At normal temperature at sea level, sound travels at a speed of about 760 miles an hour. Because of the lower air temperatures at higher altitudes, however, sound travels slower. At an altitude of 20,000 feet, for example, the speed of sound is only about 700 miles an hour; and at 36,000 feet it's 660.

At subsonic speed the air flow ahead of a plane or car is stable. But when the vehicle travels faster than the speed of sound, a different air-flow pattern results, much like a boat tossed in a storm. At such speeds, the air is compressed into a cone-like pattern called a shock wave. This extreme disturbance accumulates in a narrow region just ahead of the craft.

The shock wave travels to the ground at the speed of sound, follows the path of the plane, and becomes audible as a sonic boom as it slaps against the surface of the earth.

A symetrically-shaped plane, traveling in free air, has fewer problems traveling faster than sound, due to the equalizing of the pressures exerted on all parts.

However, this is not the case with a land-bound vehicle. The shock waves created at supersonic speed are also cone-shaped. But because of the land obstruction, the pressure exerted on the car is uneven. The top half of the car produces a negative or suction-like pressure. The bottom wave creates a positive or lifting pressure. After slamming against the ground, the shock wave has only one place to travel—up. This upward pressure could disintegrate the car or turn it into a wingless plane. Without the proper body design, a car could alternately fly and touch down.

Another major problem is thermal heat. Air

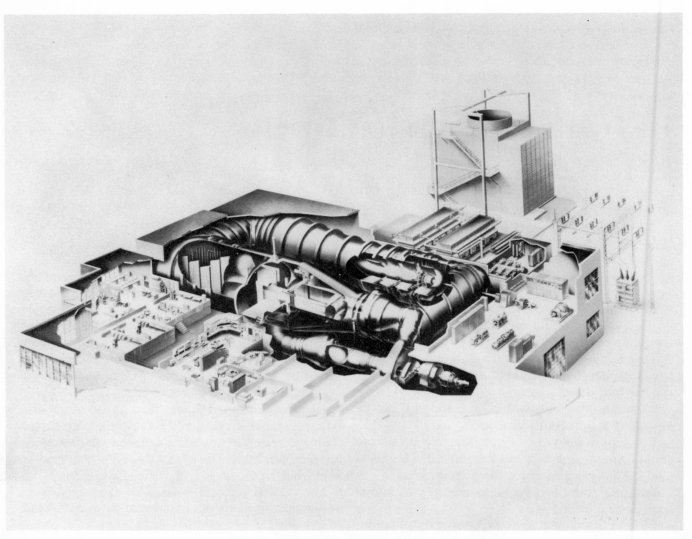

Cut-out of wind tunnel at Cornell Aeronautical Laboratory, Buffalo, N.Y. Note scale model of plane in tunnel.

flowing around a plane heats to a high temperature. For example, the air temperature in low altitude flights at Mach 3 (three times the speed of sound) would be about 940 degrees Fahrenheit. Heat holds the speed of a plane down and tends to weaken and even melt its parts.

The car must be constructed sturdily enough so that, upon entering the barrier, it can resist the pressure exerted on the front end—1,500 pounds per square foot.

What do some of the top technical minds in the aviation and auto business think about the sound barrier?

Boeing engineer John Swihart maintains, "There is no technical reason why an automobile cannot exceed the speed of sound. The only drawback would be the amount of power required.

"The main problem that faced the aircraft industry was one of designing for the airflow encountered at transsonic speeds, and in providing enough thrust to proceed through the transsonic drag rise design. They finally overcame the problem through improved aerodynamic design and better engines.

"Wind tunnel tests would be mandatory to the design of a successful land speed car. The ultimate speed limit for such a car would probably be the rotational speed limit on the wheels. The wheels will undoubtedly be the limiting factor.

"However, I cannot stress enough the importance of wind tunnel tests, because the car will have to be stable in the aerodynamic sense.

"It would undoubtedly have to have a vertical fin, like an airplane, and might also have to have longitudinal controls like an airplane."

"Theoretically, there is no reason why a land-bound vehicle could not be made to travel faster than the speed of sound," says aerospace technologist Clyde Hayes of NASA's Langley Research Center at Hampton, Virginia. Wind tunnel tests for aircrafts have been conducted at Langley for more than 40 years.

"To build a vehicle with a turbojet engine enclosed in a body, which could be similar to the nacelle of a supersonic aircraft such as a B-58, and have space for a driver and sufficient fuel to travel over a measured course would be possible.

"The problems, however, of designing a running gear that would be capable of steering and supporting such a vehicle, while regarded as only an engineering and development problem, would be a tremendous undertaking. Tires are probably a serious limiting factor at such high speeds.

To understand where such a vehicle stands in the development of high-speed transportation, we can consider first the automobile. It has many advantages over the airplane for low-speed, short range transportation.

Crooked, rough and hilly roads can be used instead of airports with long, smooth runways, and in the event of mechanical difficulties, it can be safely stopped and weather is less of a problem than with an airplane.

"As the speed is increased, the dynamic pressure (pressure due to the wind velocity relative to the vehicle) increases and the aerodynamic forces increase.

"It would be logical to utilize the aerodynamic forces to stabilize the vehicle by means of tail surfaces, and perhaps to assist in steering by means of a rudder.

"Also, to keep the vehicle on the ground so that it can be steered, the aerodynamic forces would be used to create negative lift either through the body shape or a horizontal surface or both.

"It is more logical, however, to utilize the aerodynamic forces to create lift, rise off the ground, and solve all of the more serious problems involved in a high-speed vehicle.

"Thus, the airplane is a more practical high-speed vehicle, since with high speed the advan-

tages of the automobile disappear. For instance, as the automobile speeds are increased, smoother and straighter roads are required and for very high speed it would require roads that could be used for an airplane to take off and land.

A model of the Lockheed L-1011, slated for airliner use in the 1970s, during tests in Cornell aeronautical Laboratory's Transonic wind tunnel. CAL's wind tunnel, which can generate an air stream speed of 1,000 miles per hour, has been used to test scale models of virtually every commercial and military aircraft developed in the United States in the last 23 years. CAL's transonic tunnel is one of a few in the United States available to other research organizations, defense and government agencies, as well as manufacturers, for testing of aircraft and missiles.

"Consequently, the bulk of the research has gone in this direction and the problems of the design of high-speed land vehicles are being considered only by a relatively few individuals concerned with the setting of speed records only for the sake of being able to claim such records.

"Generally, the rules used to define a land vehicle for setting a record would require that engineering problems be solved that are generally eliminated by leaving the ground.

"With regard to wind tunnel testing, the most common application of such tests is to determine the aerodynamic characteristics of a configuration. This generally consists of the forces, lift, drag and sideforce, and the movements about the three axes: pitch, yaw and roll.

"Such tests of a high-speed vehicle would be of value, but the tests would be complicated by the interference forces caused by the vehicle traveling near the ground. It should be remembered that wind tunnel testing can solve only a part of the problem, and the running gear must be tested by other means.

"Wind tunnel tests can provide the downward forces and sideforces on the wheels to aid in the design, but the problems involved in the design of the running gear remain the greatest problem.

"The final test of the running gear would be in the actual high-speed runs. Thus, to use caution, initial tests would be run slowly, gradually increasing speed while observing the steering ability and potential instabilities of the vehicle.

"This would be the case through the transsonic speed range, where part of the flow about the vehicle is subsonic and part supersonic, with unstable and transient shock waves on the vehicle.

"Aerodynamically, it would be better to accelerate rapidly through the transsonic range to some low supersonic speed at which the airflow would be stable.

"The problems involved at the time that supersonic flight was first attempted were the limited thrust of the engines available, and the drag rise encountered at transsonic speeds.

"Although they could not accelerate rapidly through transsonic speeds, even in vertical dives, sufficient speeds were attained to encounter unstable flow and transient shock waves, resulting in such phenomena as control reversal and buffeting.

"The X-I and present-day supersonic airplanes are capable of accelerating rapidly through the transsonic speed range and are not required to maneuver at such speeds. Thus, these difficulties are avoided.

"It can be said that a land vehicle that can travel at supersonic speeds, while being theoretically possible, presents two difficult engineering problems, and the entire project represents a rather dangerous undertaking."

In the opinion of Bradford A. Evans of NASA's Ames Research Center at Moffett Field, California, "The primary problem involved in a landbound car in such a speed regime is that friction between air molecules and the surfaces of the car would cause a high rate of resistance.

"At about Mach .7, or 532 miles per hour, in standard atmosphere at sea level, the air in front of the car begins to be compressed and propelled forward in a shock wave. This would result in enormous drag on the car. By sweeping back the wing of an airplane with a pointed nose, the shock waves are kept ahead of the lifting surfaces.

"The design of the car would have to be such that aerodynamic lifting forces would be at a point low enough to prevent the car from becoming 'airborne,' and thus eliminating it from the landbound category. And, of course, while airborne, it would have no directional, lateral, or vertical control, unless designed for these factors."

Alan Pope is director of aerothermodynamics at Sandia Laboratories at Albuquerque, New Mexico and a well-known expert on wind tunnel automobile testing. He has written a book, *Low-Speed Wind Tunnel Testing*.

"All of the large automobile manufacturers currently have wide tunnels available in which they test every body model and frequently every engine to go in them. These tests are largely to test engine overheating at high speed.

"Tests of racing cars are essential to determine their pitch-up conditions so that the driver may be satisfied that the nose is not going to come up and tumble end-over-end. The tests are not 100 percent accurate but they are very, very good.

"Besides giving an answer to the pitch-up problem, they do fairly well in predicting the drag, and hence, the racing car's top speed, because aerodynamic drag becomes very important—in fact it is an overwhelming item above a couple hundred miles an hour.

"The problem with wind tunnel testing of automobiles is that it really requires a moving belt under the car to simulate the motion between the ground and the car.

"It is also customary to measure yawing movements to ascertain that the car will have adequate directional stability. Many of the current vanes that racing cars have to help hold them down are tested in wind tunnels. These tests would also be very accurate.

"While I suspect that a number of very high-speed cars have been built without wind tunnel tests, their safety would be greatly enhanced by preassuring their stability.

"Finally, there is nothing mysterious about the sound barrier and I feel certain that automobiles will one day be driven through it. I would be much more concerned about keeping my tires together than I would be about the integrity of the car and the engine.''

Experts at McDonnell Douglas Aircraft take a different view.

According to H.K. Gagos, ''the consensus of our aerodynamists is that it would be extremely hazardous under present knowledge, highly improbable for an automobile, as currently known, to attain supersonic speed.

''Let's begin with the significance of the sound barrier. The speed of sound is the speed at which

Dr. John Lee, who tested scale model of ''Blue Flame'' at Ohio State University wind tunnel. *Courtesy American Gas Association.*

The ''Blue Flame'' being tested in Ohio State University wind tunnel. *Courtesy American Gas Association.*

''For an automobile, the biggest problems would be lack of stability, control and traction. It would require a shape which not only could penetrate the sound barrier, but could, at the same time, generate strong negative lift.

molecules of air can be moved. As you approach their maximum velocity, the air compresses to form a formidable and what was once considered an impenetrable wall.

''The application of theory, and experiments with such aircraft as the D-558 ''Skyrocket,'' among others, taught aircraft builders the shape of the vehicle which can best get through the barrier,—provided enough power was available.

''The trick was to develop a form on which local supersonic velocities were reached at different chronological times so that the entire mass was not retarded simultaniously. Once through the 'barrier,' flight again is smooth and ralatively undisturbed.

Aerodynamics consultant, Professor T. Paul Torda of Illinois Institute of Technology, inspects a 1/25 scale model of the ''Blue Flame'' in the supersonic wind tunnel. Velocities above Mach 1.2 were simulated in the Ohio State University facility. *Courtesy American Gas Association.*

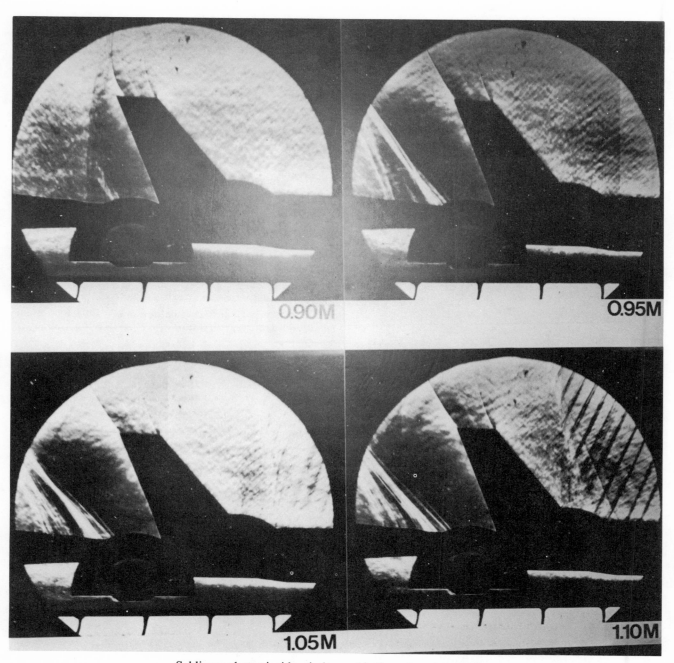

Schlieren photos inside wind tunnel indicated model of "Blue Flame" was stable. The shadows are air flowing over model. 1.10M is 920 mph. (M stands for Mach). *Courtesy American Gas Association.*

"The air should force the car downward. It is obvious, then, that wind tunnel testing would be mandatory for a vehicle of this kind. In fact, it would be imprudent not to test any high speed racing car, not only to reduce the tremendous drag but to maintain lateral stability."

Kenneth Norris, designer of Donald Campbell's jet boats and land speed car, feels "The length of the course available demands high acceleration and heavy braking.

"The primary requirements, therefore, are for a vehicle having high thrust-to-weight ratio (and high tire-to-ground friction coefficient in the case of an automobile), low resistance-to-weight ratio and a reliable means of reducing speed rapidly.

"From previous experience, even for jet-propelled vehicles, the length of the course may be between 8 and 12 miles. Assuming an average course length of 10 miles is available and that the measured distance is placed in the optimum position—that is, the middle—then the run in from each distance is restricted to 4½ miles.

"These relatively short distances demand a vehicle capable of accelerating and of being braked at an average of at least 1 G, approximately, in order to reach a Mach number of 1.1 (840) and complete its mission successfully.

"This means, allowing for the rapid rise in aerodynamic drag through the sound barrier, that the vehicle will require a thrust of 1½ times the weight, a resistance not greater than the weight of 840 and a braking system capable of providing an average retarding force at least equal to the weight of the vehicle less the resistance.

"Under these circumstances, the complete run of 10 miles one way from the start will take about one minute, the measured distance of one kilometer and one mile taking but 2½ and 4 seconds effectively.

"It is implicit in the rules that the stability of the vehicle is such that manual control is possible throughout the speed range.

"Aerodynamic forces, depending on vehicle shape, can change considerably as the vehicle passes through the sound barrier. The shock wave associated with the sound of speed and shed from the nose may rebound back and forth from the ground so that the vehicle may indeed be 'riding' on its own shock wave.

"These aerodynamic effects may adversely affect the stability of the vehicle both in pitch and yaw, but this deterioration must be limited so that the vehicle maintains load on the ground, and in such a manner that steering is adequate.

"Indeed, if the hazard to the driver is to be at all acceptable, aerodynamic stability must be maintained independent of mechanical (tire-to-ground) stability, the suspension must be extremely stiff to maintain control over the attitude of the vehicle (small changes in incidence can considerably affect aerodynamic forces) and the surface over which the run is made must be flat to fractions of an inch over 100 yards.

"Model and full-scale wind tunnel tests must be carried out to assure that the above requirements are met. Also, to meet these requirements, the wheels of the vehicle should be relatively small and housed, as far as possible, within the body.

"That means that, in order to reach the high speed required, the wheels will need to revolve at high, and, consequently, very high centrifugal forces will be general.

"Tires designed for 400 to 500 miles per hour may disintegrate at 840. These, therefore, present a considerable problem.

"Although temperature rise due to speed is unlikely to be a problem, there being a theoretical rise at the very nose of the vehicle of 70 degrees C. only at 840, noise may cause some difficulty.

"The pressure rise through the shock wave, emenating from the nose of the order of 50 pounds per square foot, and the resulting 'sonic bang' several hundred yards away (a heavy 'sonic bang' from an airplane at 30,000 feet is about two pounds per square foot) may mean that the timekeepers and other personnel operating close to the course will advisedly wear ear plugs and lie flat on the ground as the vehicle goes by.

"Flags, which are normally used as course markers, will not take too kindly to the vehicle's passage."

The drivers, aircraft and auto experts all talked about wind tunnel testing. But what is it, in a nutshell?

Dean Richmond of Cornell Aeronautical Laboratory in Buffalo, New York, supplies the answer. (Cornell's wind tunnel, one of the most advanced in the world, has been used to test models of virtually every American military and commercial aircraft design developed since 1947).

"The tunnel is laid out in a rectangular shape so that the air within the tunnel makes a continuous circuit. The rectangle is 180 feet long and 70 feet wide.

"The high-velocity air stream, which moves past a stationary model in the test section of the wind tunnel, is created by 48 variable-pitch aluminum fan blades, each seven feet long.

"The fans, arranged in three consecutive groups of 16 each, are driven by an 11,000 horsepower electric motor. It takes about two minutes of operation for the fans to have the air moving through the tunnel at the speed of sound. A 13,000 horsepower motor is also used during operation of the tunnel to help maintain a steady flow of air through the test section, where the air would have a tendency to become blocked at the higher speed ranges.

"The test section of the tunnel is a large removable cart, which can accomodate a model eight feet long with a wing span up to four feet. Many of the models are made of wood and stainless steel.

"The data gathered during a wind tunnel test is provided by small strain gauges embedded in the model. These gauges respond to the forces applied

Phenomena in the Air Produced by a Projectile." This paper described experiments with artillery shells traveling at supersonic speeds. The photographic system was called a Schieren apparatus. *Schieren* in German means "shadow."

Seventy years after its discovery, this apparatus, which permits photographing of all sorts of shock waves and other flow phenomena involving variations of density, is now a part of the equipment of every transsonic and supersonic tunnel.

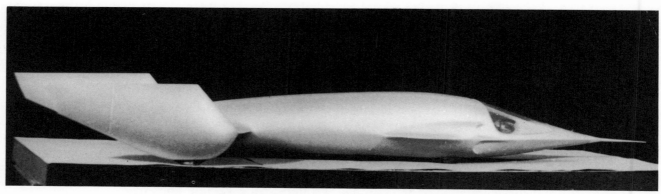

Scale model of Russian land speed car. *Courtesy Soviet Institute for Automobiles and Roads*.

to them in the wind tunnel by generating electrical pulses.

"The pulses are a measure of the amount of force being experienced by the model and are translated into specific figures on such factors as lift or drag.

"A computerized data-processing system receives the raw pulses and immediately converts them into numerical data, which engineers can analyze to determine the effectiveness or efficiency of the aircraft design.

"In addition to strain gauges, commonly used equipment includes pressure transducers, still cameras, high-speed movie cameras and shadowgraph photography."

The wind tunnel originates with Dr. Ernest Mach, an Austrian scientist, who in 1887 wrote a paper entitled "Photographic Registration of the

Mach's son, Ludwig, a physician, assisted his father in the construction of the first blow-down wind tunnel. However, it wasn't until 1950 that work on the first practical transsonic tunnel in the world had been concluded at Langley Field.

The advent of transsonic tunnels paved the way for the study of supersonic planes which could not safely be flown through the sound barrier without definite knowledge of their drag and control characteristics.

Little did Dr. Ernest Mach envision then that the wind tunnel would play a vital role in the setting of the unlimited land speed record by Gary Gabelich almost 100 years later. His "Blue Flame" was wind-tunnel tested. Valuable information from those tests helped produce the world's fastest race car.

3
The Flying Mile

What is land speed racing?

It is a test of man and machine. It is a projectile launched at speeds that only a split-second electronic timer can record. It is a lonely ride that lasts an eternity.

Until 1910, only one run was required for the land speed record. Since then, however, a driver must make two runs in opposite directions within 60 minutes for the attempt to be considered official.

In addition to the time for the measured or flying mile, the time for the kilometer is also recorded. The kilo is the final five-eighths of a mile. The times for both runs through the measured mile are calibrated, then translated into miles per hour to determine the average speed.

Man's quest for land speed records at Bonneville usually takes place early in the morning, just after dawn, when the winds are quietest and the salt the driest.

Although the track may be as long as 12 miles, only the speed through the flying mile—at the midway point—is timed. A black line, 12 inches wide and as many miles long, gives the driver a guideline.

In order to set a record, a driver must exceed the existing mark by one percent. Between land speed runs, a car is refueled, parachutes repacked and tires checked for wear.

No land speed attempts are permitted once the wind gusts exceed five miles an hour. All it takes is a blast of wind to push a car off course and trigger a catastrophe.

The sensation of speed means different things to different people. For instance:

Sir Malcolm Campbell: "It was as if the world had been reduced to a small eliptical surface, which traveled along with me. At no time could I see more than a few hundred yards down the salt."

John Cobb: "I had the odd sensation of driving up a steep hill."

Art Arfons: "When you're only three-quarters of an inch off the ground, the sensation of speed is tremendous. The land markers go by awfully fast. It takes only two miles to accelerate to over 500, so the pull on my body is tremendous."

How does a driver know he's approaching the measured mile?

Because of the speed involved, Arfons designed specially colored signs to indicate when he was entering and leaving the measured mile. In his case, the sign approaching the flying mile was painted black with a green cross. He knew he was leaving the mile by a huge sign painted with red and black checks.

The course, maintained by the Bonneville Racing Association, is 10-20 yards wide.

The United States Auto Club (USAC) conducts land speed attempts in America. The Federation Internationale de l'Automobile (FIA), based in Paris, is the international body controlling motor sports—including land speed racing.

It costs about $2,000 a day for a driver to run for the record.

Land speed racing dates back to 1898 when Count de Chasseloup-Laubat, a French count, drove his electric car through the mile in 57 seconds flat. His speed was 39.34. Chasseloup-Laubat's claim to the record incensed Carmile Jenatzy, a Belgian inventor, who knew his electric car was faster. Racing over the same straight stretch of road at Acheres, outside of Paris, bet-

Henry Ford in his special racer, with which he covered the mile, flying start, in 40 seconds. *Courtesy The Birthplace of Speed Association, Ormond Beach, Fla.*

ween the villages of St. Germain and Constans, Jenatzy wheeled to a new record of 41.42. However, before the day was over, Chasseloup-Laubat came back with an even faster 43.69 before burning out his motor.

Ormond Garage, 1905, known as the original Gasoline Alley. At left, Louis Rass in Stanley "Teakettle," which made a record 94.7 on the beach. Long-hooded car #2 is L.L. Bowdens 120 hp Mercedes, which made world's record 109.75 mph. *Courtesy The Birthplace of Speed Association.*

Jenatzy, his car's batteries exhausted, waited for 10 days before making a crack at regaining the world land speed record. He sped through the flying mile at 49.92 for the glory of Belgium.

A month later, however, the fearless Frenchman went 57.60 and Jenatzy realized that his car could never top that speed. So he returned home and designed a new bullet-shaped automobile, the first streamliner in history, and called his creation "Jamias Contente"—"Never Satisfied."

On April Fool's Day of 1899, Jenatzy and his "Never Satisfied" blazed down the road at Acheres at a record speed. But the French timers had failed to clock the run.

One month later Jenatzy returned to Acheres, lectured the timers and shattered two barriers considered as formidable as the sound barrier is today: 65.79 for the mile and 105.88 for the flying kilometer.

By 1902, Americans entered the speed game on the glistening sands of Ormond Beach, in the northern section of Daytona Beach, Florida.

At that time, guests at the luxurious Hotel Ormond engaged in the earliest beach motor car con-

34

Ormond Beach, Fla., January 1905. Left to right: #6, E.R. Thomas in a Mercedes, #1, W.K.Vanderbilt in his 90 hp Mercedes, #5, Arthur MacDonald, driving S.F. Edge's 90 hp Napier, #4, Louis Ross, in the famous Stanley "Teakettle." Winner was MacDonald at 104.65 mph, which was a world's record. He received the famous silver Miller Trophy for this win. *Courtesy The Birthplace of Speed Association.*

tests. Ranson E. Olds, pioneer auto builder, and U.S. race champion Alexander Winton, tied at 57 miles an hour in their wheel-to-wheel duel. The following year Winton hit 68 for a world record. His car is preserved at the Smithsonian institute in Washington, D.C.

This heralded the start of racing at the famed Florida strip. In the next 32 years, a total of 15 land speed records were set on the sand.

Other speed marks were set in such places at Lake St. Clair in Michigan, Nice (France), Brooklands (England), Pendine (Wales).

In 1904, Henry Ford powered his hand-built, six-cylinder "Arrow" across a frozen lake outside of Detroit at a speed of 91.370. A month later, however, William K. Vanderbilt drove his German-built Mercedes to a faster clocking — 92.307 — at Ormond Beach.

Halfway around the world, in Nice, Louis Rigolly of France became the first to shatter the 100 mile-an-hour barrier with a 103.55 clocking.

That same year in Florida, Arthur MacDonald and his six-cylinder, 90-horsepower Napier churned down Ormond Beach at 104.65. On another run, he traveled five miles in 3 minutes and 17 seconds.

In 1906, Fred Marriott gunned his Stanley Steamer "Rocket" to a blistering 127.66 at Ormond Beach, thus becoming the first man to drive an auto more than two miles a minute.

But later that year, Marriott wrecked his car. He was lucky to come out of it alive. When asked about the spectacular crash, he said: "I looked the beach over and found some depressions in the sand. This was not good, but I was determined to run anyway. So after taking a seven mile acceleration run I hit the measured mile wide open.

"I ran through the first depressions without trouble, then suddenly I hit some that felt like running into a curbstone. The car went up like a kite and I sailed through the air for 100 feet. The car broke in half when it landed and I was in the front half with my head in the water."

Several of his ribs were broken, his face cut, and one eye was hanging limply on his cheek. It marked the last time a steam-propelled car would contend for the land speed title.

From 1909 to 1920, the German-made Benz dominated the speed scene. The famed Barney Oldfield drove his "Blitzen Benz" to a two-way average of 131.72 at Ormond Beach in 1910.

Although another American driving champion,

Tommy Milton, clocked a sizzling 156.03 in 1920, his record was not officially recognized. He made only one run in his Duesenberg, powered by side-by-side 8-cylinder Duesenberg engines. Each engine drove one rear wheel through its own independent driveshaft.

Across the Atlantic, the British were readying for the challenge. The car was the famous 350 horsepower, single-seat Sunbeam, powered by a wartime aircraft engine.

The 350 hp Sunbeam first appeared at Brooklands in 1920. Two years later, K. L. Guinness reached 144 around the flying half mile at Brooklands.

On May 17, 1922, Guinness set a world land-speed record of 133.75. It was the same car that Sir Malcolm Campbell would buy and use to set the first of his nine land speed marks.

Campbell was born to set records. Even as a youngster, speed was his obsession: "When I drove my first seven horsepower car, I craved for 10. I wanted to experience the sensation of traveling faster."

Born March 11, 1885 in Chislehurst, Kent, England, Campbell showed an early enthusiasm for speed As early as 1905 he was winning medals in motorcycling events and in 1909 tried flying. Building his own airplane, he flew for a time, but successive crashes proved to be too much of a drain on his savings.

The year 1910 marked his first official automobile race at Brooklands, England's famous track, and the appearance of the name "Bluebird" for his cars. That year Campbell took a Darracq car which won the Vanderbilt Cup in America the year before, painted it blue and went to Brooklands to win his race.

Entering World War I soon after the declaration of hostilities, he became a dispatch rider, then was made a commissioned officer. He transferred to the Royal Flying Corps and was discharged in 1919 with the rank of captain.

He immediately re-entered the racing field, taking part in many contests, and then, fired by the record speed of 142 miles an hour set in 1911 by "Wild Bob" Burman at Ormond Beach, he began his campaign to make the world mark his own. The best European mark was then 109, made by Georges Boillot in 1914.

Campbell never talked of what speed he might make, but his wife admitted that 300 miles an hour was his goal. His first assault on the land speed record was made with a borrowed car in 1922 at Saltburn-On-Sea, Yorkshire. He averaged 135, but the mark wasn't accepted because the speed had been timed by a hand-held stop watch instead of by the electrical timing device required by official rules.

Barney Oldfield in the "Blitzen Benz" at Ormond Beach, Fla., in March 1910, where he set a world's record of 131.724 mph. The car had a four-cylinder, 200 hp motor and 112-inch wheelbase. *Courtesy The Birthplace of Speed Association.*

At that time, K. Lee Guinness, also of England, held the official record at 133.75.

A year later, after having purchased Guinness' 350-horsepower Sunbeam, Campbell entered the international speed trials at Fanoe, Denmark, and on June 24, 1923, reached 137 miles an hour. Again he failed to win recognition, because of the type of timing apparatus.

Twice, he had bettered the existing record, but twice his efforts were rejected.

In July of 1924, the record eluded him at Fanoe when his tires flew off. Undaunted, he took the car to Pendine Sands, on the coast of Wales. By then he had been joined by three other challengers, including 1914 Indianapolis "500" winner Rene Thomas of France and J.G. Parry Thomas and E.A.D. Eldridge, both from England.

On July 6, Thomas clocked 143.26 at Arpajon in France for a new two-way record. Four days later, Eldridge upped the mark to 143.8. However, Thomas lodged a protest, claiming that Eldridge's car was not fitted with a reverse gear, as was required by international rules. Within 48 hours a reverse gear was fitted on the six-cylinder Fiat. This time, Thomas could only watch as Eldridge clocked an even faster 145.897. This time there was no protest.

IN ORMOND BEACH

"Birthplace of Speed"

BEACH RACING BEGAN HERE IN 1902

EARLY RECORDS

1902 R.E. OLDS AND ALEXANDER WINTON TIED 57 M.P.H.
1903 BARNEY OLDFIELD 67 M.P.H.— W.K. VANDERBILT 92.307 M.P.H.
1905 ARTHUR McDONALD 104.65 — 1905 H.L. BOWDEN 109.75 M.P.
1906 FRED MARRIOTT 127.65 M.P.H.— 1906 GLENN CURTIS

OTHER PARTICIPITANTS

LOUIS CHEVROLET · · HENRY FORD · · RALPH DePALMA
TOMMY MILTON · · H.O.E. SEAGRAVE · · SIR MALCOM CAMPBELL
RAY KETCH

Historical marker overlooking world's first beach race
course. "Fireball" Roberts, famous NASCAR driving champion, displays one of his trophies. *Courtesy The Birthplace of
Speed Association.*

4

"Jolly Good Show, Old Chap"

Prestige is more than just a word to an English-man. It's a way of life. It was the driving force that motivated men like Malcolm Campbell to risk their lives for the sake of a land speed record.

Even in 1933, when Campbell traveled 272.463 miles an hour at Ormond Beach in Florida, the nerveless, daring and romantic Englishman wasn't satisfied.

"I cannot rest on my laurels," he said. "I will go on until I am too old to drive—and I am not too old yet. That time may come soon, however, perhaps in a year or two, and for the sake of British prestige I want to raise the record as high as possible while I am still capable of doing so."

From 1924 through 1947, British drivers set 23 land speed records. Only once was their string broken, when Ray Keech of the United States averaged 207.55 in his Triplex on April 22, 1928.

The string began with E.A.D. Eldridge and his Fiat.

During that span, Campbell set nine records, the first on September 25, 1924, when he averaged 146.16 through the driving rain at Pendine Sands.

Campbell had wanted to become the first to travel 200 miles an hour, but fellow countryman Henry Seagrave beat him to the punch with a blistering 203.79 performance in Florida.

Until then, the so-called "experts" said a car would break up at speeds in excess of 200 miles an hour—that the wheels would fly off, or the cars would take off and fly.

Seagrave proved otherwise by becoming the first to travel three miles a minute.

Campbell began to rebuild his "Bluebird." He obtained a Schneider trophy seaplane engine,

equipped his machine with a rear fish-tail fin to stabilize it, and added wheel fairings.

On February 19, 1929, at Ormond Beach, he achieved a new record of 206.96, but his triumph was short-lived, for Keech boosted the mark to 207.55.

While Campbell went to Verneuk Pan, a dried lake bed 400 miles from Cape Town, South Africa, Seagrave and his "Golden Arrow" left for Florida. Seagrave that year boosted the record to 231.36. The best Campbell could do in South Africa was 218.5, but he set new records for the five kilometer and five-mile distances.

Major Seagrave, who had been knighted, turned his back on land speed in a quest for the water speed record. He was killed when his boat hit a submerged log in a Scottish lake.

Campbell spent most of 1930 remodeling his "Bluebird." The car was given a new body and a new engine, a 1,450 horsepower Schneider racing type. He returned to Florida and on February 5, 1931, covered the flying mile at 246.153 miles an hour.

England went wild. The returning hero was still on board ship when he was notified that a knight-hood had been granted him.

He still wasn't satisfied. Soon after he added another to his long list of narrow escapes when the steering rod of another car he was driving at Brooklands broke.

"Bluebird" was altered again. It was given new streamlining and an engine of the same type, but developing slightly more horsepower. He re-turned to Ormond Beach and on February 24, 1932, drove at 253.96.

Returning to England, he once more rebuilt the car. When it was completed nine months later, the car was longer, heavier and more powerful. A new streamlined body had been fitted. And under the hood was a 12 cylinder 2500 horsepower engine.

With this machine he set his 1933 record of 272.463.

When the glistening sands of Ormond Beach had outlived their usefulness, Campbell searched for a longer and harder surface. He found it at the Bonneville Salt Flats.

On September 3, 1935, he fulfilled his goal with a 301.13 average. His first run through the measured mile lasted 11.63 seconds, or 304,311. The trip southward lasted 12.08 seconds, or 298.013 MPH.

Sir Malcolm Campbell was happy, but weary. "The old car stood up beautifully. I couldn't have expected more. Now it's going home with me...we're both going to rest."

Sir Malcolm Campbell in the "Bluebird" at Ormond Beach, March, 1935. He set a world's record of 276.82 mph. Car was powered by a Rolls Royce V-12, 2500 hp engine. *Courtesy The Birthplace of Speed Association.*

Then he added: "No, I have not set a record I cannot beat. I can build a car that will go much faster, and I shall probably do that. Nor have I set

Sir Malcolm Campbell breaks 300 mph barrier at Bonneville Salt Flats in 1935. *Courtesy Deseret News.*

Malcolm Campbell's "Bluebird" No. 2. *Courtesy Clayton L. Gontner.*

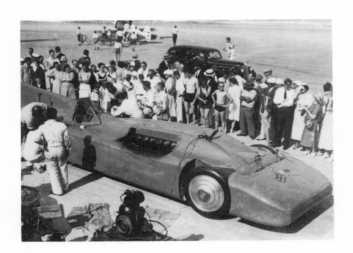

"Bluebird" No. 5, 1935, at Ormond Beach. Spectators crowd beach to see Malcolm Campbell run for record. *Courtesy Clayton L. Gontner.*

Line print of construction of "Bluebird" No. 5, 1935. *Courtesy Clayton L. Gontner.*

In the cutaway drawing displayed herewith the skeleton structure of steel tubing which carries the panelling is shown, but the panelling itself has been omitted in order to reveal the mechanical details. The shape of the completed car is made clear by the sketch reproduced in connection with the cutaway drawing. It will be noticed that the fairings extend to the full width over the wheels and wind-tunnel tests have shown this shape to be most effective in reducing windage. Another novel feature is the provision of a control by which the driver can close the air intake to the radiator, so as to improve the streamline flow when covering the measured mile.

A supercharged Rolls-Royce engine of the famous Schneider Trophy type is again employed and the gearbox and clutch remain unchanged. New transmission features include the use of twin rear wheels and a duplicated final drive, details of which are given on the opposite page.

The immense strength of the frame will be noticed; the side members pass beneath the rear axle and are upswept forward of the engine to clear the front axle. The latter component is controlled by radius arms. The car is carried by semi-elliptic springs, damped by powerful frictional shock absorbers. The driver's seat is mounted in a low position alongside an offset torque tube.

To cope with the relatively short distance available for retardation after covering the measured mile, the mechanical braking system is supplemented by air flaps which are operated by a large vacuum servo cylinder mounted in the tail. These rise out of the recesses into the airstream when the brake pedal is depressed and create a downward thrust on the rear wheels in addition to producing an effective resistance to motion. Full details of this most interesting car are published on the opposite page.

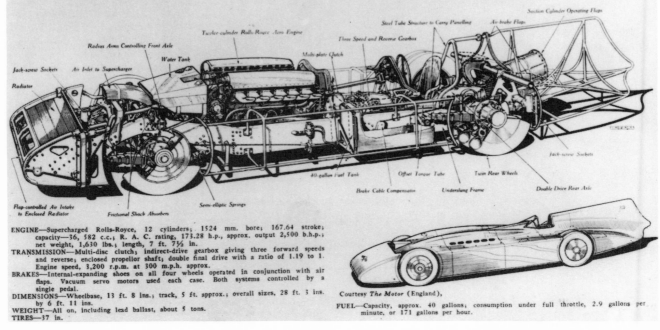

ENGINE—Supercharged Rolls-Royce, 12 cylinders; 1524 mm. bore; 167.64 stroke; capacity—36, 582 c.c.; R. A. C. rating, 173.28 h.p., approx. output 2,500 b.h.p.; net weight, 1,630 lbs.; length, 7 ft. 7½ in.
TRANSMISSION—Multi-disc clutch; indirect-drive gearbox giving three forward speeds and reverse; enclosed propeller shaft; double final drive with a ratio of 1.19 to 1. Engine speed, 3,200 r.p.m. at 300 m.p.h. approx.
BRAKES—Internal-expanding shoes on all four wheels operated in conjunction with air flaps. Vacuum servo motors used each case. Both systems controlled by a single pedal.
DIMENSIONS—Wheelbase, 13 ft. 8 ins.; track, 5 ft. approx.; overall sizes, 28 ft. 3 ins. by 6 ft. 11 ins.
WEIGHT—All on, including lead ballast, about 5 tons.
TIRES—37 in.

Courtesy *The Motor* (England).

FUEL—Capacity, approx. 40 gallons; consumption under full throttle, 2.9 gallons per minute, or 171 gallons per hour.

Chassis of "Bluebird" No. 5. *Courtesy Clayton L. Gontner.*

Malcolm Campbell's "Bluebird" No. 1 at Pendine Sands in
1927. *Courtesy Clayton L. Gontner.*

Ab Jenkins' famed "Mormon Meteor." *Courtesy Firestone Tire & Rubber Co.*

a record that another driver can't beat. No man could do that, for what I can do another man can do."

How fast could a man travel on land?

"Given the right surface, a long enough run, and a car designed for the work, a man may even reach 500 miles an hour. The limiting factor to ultimate speed will be the difficulty of finding a suitable course, not in the cars themselves or in the human element."

Sir Malcolm Campbell had achieved all had set out to do on land, so he turned his attention to the water and went on to set four records between 1937 and 1939.

Shortly before he died on January 1, 1949, Campbell had been experimenting with a jet-propelled speedboat.

His "Bluebird" is on permanent display at the

Museum of Speed in Daytona Beach, Florida. The "Bluebird" is 30 feet long and weighs five tons. It was powered by a special 2,500 horsepower, V-12 engine, the most powerful ever installed in a car. The engine alone cost the British government more than $75,000. Specially-built tires with a life of just seven minutes cost $1800 each.

The "Bluebird," which used three gallons of gas a minute, had three speeds and could run 175 miles an hour in low gear. It is only three feet high at the cockpit and the driver's seat is just 18 inches off the ground. The highest part of the car is the top of the stabilizing tail fin, which is five feet high.

No car built anywhere in the world and powered by one engine driving through a conventional transmission and rear end has traveled as fast as Malcolm Campbell's legendary "Bluebird."

While one Englishman faded from the land

John Cobb of England. *Courtesy Deseret News, Salt Lake City, Utah.*

John Cobb's "Railton Special" at Bonneville Salt Flats during record run in 1947. *Courtesy Deseret News, Salt Lake City, Utah.*

Barney Oldfield (left) and Sir Malcolm Campbell confer just before one of Campbell's historic runs at Daytona Beach. *Courtesy The Birthplace of Speed Association.*

"Bluebird" in action. *Courtesy The Birthplace of Speed Association.*

Sir Malcolm Campbell checks the tires of the massive "Bluebird." *Courtesy The Birthplace of Speed Association.*

In 1905 Arthur MacDonald and his 6-cylinder Napier hit an astounding 104.65 mph at Ormond Beach, Fla. *Courtesy The Birthplace of Speed Association.*

speed picture, two others picked up the gauntlet.

John Cobb and Captain George Eyston waged a fierce battle between 1938 and 1939.

Eyston began his speed pursuits in 1923 in European road races. Later, he set numerous distance records in his car, "Speed of the Wind." On November 19, 1937, the shy, retiring driver piloted his 10-wheel, 7-ton "Thunderbolt" to a new land speed mark of 311.42.

Less than a year later—August 27, 1938—Eyston upped his speed to 345.50. "Thunderbolt," painted black to overcome a glaring sun, hit 347.49 on its outward trip and 343.41 on the return jaunt.

"Thunderbolt was by no means at full throttle on either run," he said. "I had a very comfortable ride and not once did I feel there was any danger. I'm getting rather used to the sensation of high speed now. I seem to go through that measured mile like it was a mere 100 yards. Things fly at you

R.E. Olds (pictured) and Alexander Winton, pioneer automobile manufacturers, were the first to race at Ormond Beach in 1902. They clocked identical 57 mph speeds in a wheel-to-wheel duel. *Courtesy The Birthplace of Speed Association.*

Alexander Winton. *Courtesy The Birthplace of Speed Association.*

tremendously fast. The sensation I used to have when I first went over 300 is wearing off. I don't feel as though the salt is curving down in front of the car and I'm going downhill. I just seem to be whistling through space. I really don't have much time to think about sensations.''

Two weeks later, Cobb smashed Eyston's record with a 350.20 performance in his turtle-shaped ''Railton Special.''

No sooner had Cobb begun enjoying the fruits of his victory than Eyston powered his mammoth, 24-cylinder creation to a new two-way average of 357.50. The land speed record had been shattered twice within 24 hours.

Eyston held the record for a year. On August 23, 1939, John Cobb streaked across the Bonneville Salt Flats at a 368.90 mph clip.

During World War II, Cobb was in the Royal Air Force, serving as a ferry pilot in the British Air Transport Auxiliary.

In 1947, at the age of 47, the fur broker from London returned to Utah. Except for minor

changes, the ''Railton Special'' was essentially the same car that had smashed the world land speed record eight years before.

On September 16, 1947, Cobb started the two engines, working up 1250 horsepower apiece. Slowly the car gained momentum.

Cobb's first run through the measured mile was 385.645. It was fast, but not fast enough to suit him.

Less than an hour later, John Cobb began his south-to-north return run. In the span of nine seconds he had blasted through the flying mile. Official speed: 403.135. His peak speed at one point was 415.

Cobb's two-way average was 394.196 for the mile and 393.836 for the kilometer. It had taken him seven long weeks to break the record.

Asked how it felt to drive at 400 miles an hour, Cobb replied laconically: ''It feels bloody quick.''

While Cobb wanted to go faster, two factors prevented any further runs, the condition of the car and the weather.

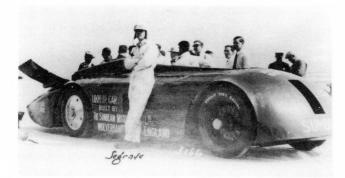

Henry Seagrave of England with Sunbeam, 1927. He was the first man to travel at 200 mph. *Courtesy The Birthplace of Speed Association.*

Indianapolis "500" winner Ralph DePalma also tried his hand at land speed racing at Ormond Beach. *Courtesy The Birthplace of Speed Association.*

Glenn Curtiss, riding a hand-built motorcycle, went better than two miles a minute at Ormond Beach in 1907. *Courtesy The Birthplace of Speed Association.*

Tommy Milton and Duesenberg, 1920. *Courtesy The Birthplace of Speed Association.*

"Owing to the terrific punishment the car has taken for the many tests required preceeding this run, it has been decided not to risk further serious damage which might possibly result from any attempts to establish records for five miles and ten miles."

Despite setting the record, Cobb called it "the roughest ride I have yet had on the Salt Flats. It felt like I was riding inside an infuriated vibration machine."

Less than 24 hours later a heavy rainfall flooded the flats to a depth of 2-6 inches.

Reid Railton, Cobb's long-time friend and creater of the British car, felt there was probably another 60 miles an hour left in his creation.

Cobb agreed. "I think the topmost speed for an automobile lies somewhere between 400 and 450 miles. Tires just won't stand up under the heat generated by friction in speed much above 400." The "Railton Special's" (Dunlop) tire treads were almost paper-thin.

In 1949, the speed specialist said: "I don't think I'll be very active in high-speed work any more. The record? I've got it. I won't bother again unless someone else breaks it."

Like Henry Seagrave and Malcolm Campbell before him, John Cobb then turned his attention to the world water speed record. And like Seagrave he met his death on water. Cobb was killed on September 29, 1952 when his jet-powered boat exploded at more than 200 miles an hour.

Technically speaking, there are presently two reigning land speed kings—Gary Gabelich (622.407) and Bobby Summers (409.277).

Fred Marriott in Stanley Steamer. He hit 127.6 mph in 1907.
Courtesy The Birthplace of Speed Association.

Gabelich set his record in a rocket car, propelled entirely by thrust. Summers, however, took the old-fashioned approach and built a four-wheeler, with the power transmitted directly through the wheels.

Thus, there are the pure thrust and wheel-driven classes.

Kenneth Norris, designer of the late Donald Campbell's "Bluebird," which held the wheel-driven record of 403.1 (although powered by a jet engine, 40 percent of the power was transmitted through the wheels) until Summers went six miles an hour faster, explained how the rule change which allowed for two unlimited classes came about.

"After Donald Campbell obtained the world record—in July 1964—the FIA agreed to accept claims for world records for a special class of vehicles having at least four wheels, being propelled otherwise than through the wheels, two of which must be responsible for direction, although propulsion and direction must both be controlled by a person on board the vehicle.

"Thus, although the definition of 'automobile' remains the same and Bob Summers of California holds the world record for automobiles, the out-and-out land speed record, as the public now understands it, can be taken by a vehicle employing jet or rocket propulsion, thus avoiding the transmission problem which severely handicaps the automobile.

"Also the FIA and International Motorcycle Federation (FIM) have jointly agreed to recognize a land speed record, a vehicle of four wheels or

George Eyston of England, who battled countryman John Cobb in 1938-39 at Bonneville Salt Flats. Eyston's massive "Thunderbolt" hit 350 mph. *Courtesy Montague Motor Museum, Beaulieu, Great Britain.*

more coming within the province of the FIA and a vehicle with one, two or three wheels coming within the province of the FIM.

"This means that the land speed record can be taken by a vehicle having any number of wheels, and the title is apparently open to a vehicle having no wheels, provided that it is dependent upon the ground for its support during the record run.

"Apart from Bob Summers' successful effort, most Americans have turned from attempting the land speed record with automobiles to the much easier task of taking the record with jet or rocket propelled vehicles.

"Speeds have risen to the point where the next worthwhile challenge on land, both technically and from the driver's point of view, is the breaking of the sound barrier."

The remains of Fred Marriott's 1907 crash at Ormond Beach. *Courtesy The Birthplace of Speed Association.*

5
Death—A Constant Companion

The cockpit is barely large enough to fit a driver. Yet death is always a constant companion.

Since 1960, two men have been killed during land speed attempts. Five others survived brushes with disaster.

On August 1, 1960, Athol Graham fired up his "City of Salt Lake." Two miles into his run, the blood-red car went airborne and crashed. Graham, 36, died two hours later at a Salt Lake City hospital.

On September 10, 1962, Glenn Leasher had already made one ride in Romeo Palamides' jet-thrust "Infinity."

On his second burst, Leasher reached a speed of 250 miles an hour when the jet car appeared to blow up. The car crashed, killing Leasher.

The late Donald Campbell, Dr. Nathan Ostich, Craig Breedlove, Art Arfons and current land speed king Gary Gabelich all flirted with death on the Bonneville Salt Flats.

Campbell sustained a broken ear drum, ruptured middle ear, and skull fracture as a result of his spectacular 360 mile an hour slide in 1960. He blamed "oxygen poisoning" for the crash.

"I knew she was going out of control. Felt it. Actually felt the tail spinning. And I knew what would happen. I knew I'd crash but none of it seemed to concern me. I just sat there in that split second thinking 'well, this is the end.' And not feeling the remotest interest."

Campbell breathed pure oxygen at Bonneville.

"As we discovered much later, there are certain people—and I of course had to be one of them—who experienced a form of drunkenness if they inhale pure oxygen at sea level."

Following that discovery, carbon dioxide was mixed with oxygen.

Four years later the dogged Englishman drove the same "Bluebird" to a world land speed record for wheel-driven cars—403.1—at Lake Eyre, Australia.

Ostich, a Los Angeles doctor who ushered in the jet age in 1960 with his "Flying Caduceus," skidded out of control after hitting 331 in 1962. Fortunately, damage to both the driver and car was slight.

In 1964, Breedlove survived his wild ride after setting a two-way unlimited thrust mark of 526. His three-wheeled "Spirit of America" splintered a row of telephone poles and finally ended up nose first in a small lake. Breedlove swam to safety.

One year later Breedlove's second jet—Spirit of America-Sonic I—gave the colorful Californian another scare when it went airborne at 600 miles an hour.

Art Arfons, who battled Breedlove for two years, miraculously escaped death on November 17, 1966, when his 17,500-horsepower "Green Monster" crashed at an estimated 610. Arfons official clocking through the flying mile was 585.

While the home-made jet car was a total loss, Arfons suffered only salt burns, facial cuts and bruises. Not one broken limb.

On October 11, 1970—12 days before he set the unlimited thrust record—Gabelich rode out a 550 mile an hour ride which ended 13½ miles from the starting point and some four miles past where he had intended to bring "The Blue Flame" to a halt.

"It was a weird feeling," he recalls. "I tripped the toggle on the parachute, then waited for the impact when it opened. Nothing happened so I tripped the emergency chute. When nothing happened the second time I knew I was going a long way.

"I just flipped on the intercom and told the crew to come and get me. Man, it was shaky for a time. I tried to steer left toward the mountains, but the car kept skidding to the right. My main concern was that the right wheel would dig into the salt and cause the car to roll.

"Finally, I skidded to a halt and all of a sudden the weird thought that my chutes hadn't deployed struck me. It struck me very funny. The "Flame" was covered with salt when it stopped. You'd have thought we were sponsored by Morton's the way it looked."

All of these men knew the danger involved in the high-speed game, yet they all risked their lives. Why?

Campbell once said, "There is no escape from record breaking, and I know perfectly well that no record can ever be final. Once you have had a taste of a record bid you can never get away from it. It will be a sorry day when we no longer do something for the hell of it."

Ego, Campbell thought, played a major factor in his pursuing land and water speed records.

"You know why I do this? Conceit," he said. "No other reason when you boil it down. The conceit of believing that this is something I can do better than anyone else in the world.

"I suppose it's the same with most artists or politicians. Everyone likes to think that they're unique. This is my way of proving it."

Campbell admitted that he had never met anyone who wasn't afraid of death, including himself.

"At the same time one must keep the thing in perspective. One must realize that this is a very natural fear that the good Lord has built into every living creature, and that it is possible, as many people do, to grossly exaggerate it.'

He was killed January 4, 1967, in an attempt to better his own water-speed record. Donald Campbell was 45.

For Campbell and Arfons, the love of speed was inherited. Sir Malcolm Campbell set nine land speed and three water-speed records. The son picked up where his legendary father had left off.

Arfons recalls his early days:

"My dad had a Pierce-Arrow and he used to like speed. I got it from him. He used to have that car

fixed up where it'd go over 100, and that was back in the 1920s.

"I used to drive a truck a little hard and he'd have guys come back and say that I was going this fast or that fast and he'd say, 'Well, he takes care of the truck and if he burns it up he'll fix it.' My dad never did raise hell with em."

Volunteer associate checks out 35-year-old Graham, father of four children, in homemade "City of Salt Lake," before starting speed run. Car used 140-octane gas, was equipped with unorthodox pressed-steel truck wheels, conventional brake and drum assemblies. Canopy is from P-51 Mustang. *Courtesy Firestone Tire & Rubber Company.*

The surge of power turns Art Arfons on, so to speak.

"Them old Allison engines sure done something to me. They just sounded power. You could feel the piston engine vibrate the frames."

Later, he set three jet unlimited records in a 17,500 horsepower volcano that rumbled and spewed a fiery ball.

Arfons feels a mental change takes place when he slides into the coffin-tight cockpit: "Climbing into the car they tell me I'm white as a ghost. Then the motor winds up and it's a Jekyll and Hyde sort of thing. The whine becomes music and all I want to do is put my foot through the floorboards."

Speed is his obsession.

"I think mountain climbing and land-speed racing come under the category of sports. How many guys get killed in football each year? Why do they go out and run back and forth across the field to see who can get to the other end?

"Courage of Australia" after its record-breaking run at Orange County International Raceway. *Courtesy Mirror Newspapers Limited, Sydney, Australia.*

"Financially, I haven't made money out of land speed racing. So why do I do it? I don't know how to explain it. It's really something I don't understand myself. Maybe because it's there.

"Everything is running on the ragged edge and it's just like you're balancing yourself. A couple of ounces can push you off

"It's almost like playing Russian Roulette. The more times you pull the trigger, the more chances you have of being wiped out. I know I'll never survive another 600 mile-an-hour crash…"

What does five-time world land speed record holder Craig Breedlove have to say about the high-speed game he plays?

"A lot of people probably think I'm crazy to drive a car faster than a rifle shot, just so I can say I hold the world land speed record. Some people think I drive too fast in a conventional car as well.

"On the road, I drive fast because I want to get there. At Bonneville, I drive the way I do because I have the desire to win, to be on top."

Breedlove, like the others, fully realizes the dangers.

"If something goes wrong at 600 you've really got problems. And the faster we go, the greater the danger.

"Driving at 600 miles an hour is very demanding, both physically and psychologically. You've got 8000 pounds of car going faster than a 30-30 bullet, or a cruising jet airliner.

"Once I close the canopy, it's all business. You've got a tiger by the tail and you'd better hang on.

"The pressure acceleration is about 2 Gs—not too severe. But it gets as high as 10 Gs when the drag chute goes out. You just hang on there in your seat belt. It feels as though the car is tipped over on its nose and you're driving upside down."

While the money is nice, Breedlove's main motivation is prestige.

"Lets's face it. When you sit down in that cockpit, all the money in the world isn't going to make you drive that car if you don't really want the record.

goes from zero to 650. At 600 my hearing goes completely. I'm up to 630 when I hit the measured mile.

"It's no longer man and machine. I'm part of 'The Blue Flame,' I smell the heat of the engine, of the wires. At the half-way point it's 650. I'm all out of fuel. I release the first parachute. My head is thrown forward.

"I'm pulling 7 Gs. The blood is rushing to the top of my head like a waterfall. At 250, I release the second chute. I'm thrown forward again. The safety straps tear into my shoulders. At 150, I hit the brakes, turn off the cameras, tape recorders, everything. It's fantastic, unreal."

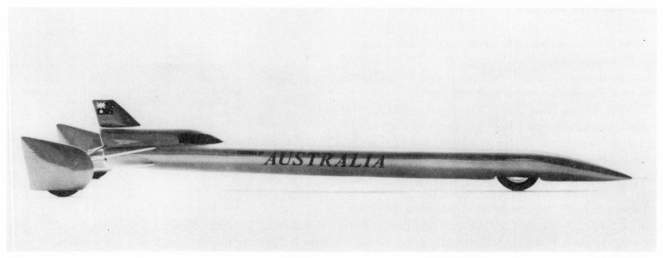

Model of supersonic land-speed record attempt car, "Courage of Australia."*Courtesy Mirror Newspapers Limited, Sydney, Australia.*

"Believe it or not, speed really scares the stuffing out of me. I certainly don't crave it."

What's it like to travel 622 MPH? Gabelich explains:

"After I calm down the adrenalin starts pumping and I'm thinking clear and sharp. I enter a complete world of my own, like I'm self-hypnotized. I push the throttle to the floor and my head is forced back hard.

"I'm looking through a small window, straight ahead at the markers where the measured mile begins, calling out my speeds into a mike in my oxygen mask. In 22 seconds 'The Blue Flame'

Gabelich admits there's no rational explanation for what he does.

"Speed, the feeling of going fast, had been part of my life ever since I can remember. I guess it's doing something a lot of people can't do or refuse to.

"I've always had the secret dream to hold the land-speed record. There's no greater feeling than being a winner. It would be exciting and groovy to go to the moon, but I like racing too much to give it up for that. Land on the moon and you're a hero for one day. Set the land-speed record and you're a hero for the rest of your life.

"Racing has been good to me. It's my livelihood, my whole existence. Sure, I accept the dangers involved. It's part of my profession."

Gabelich speaks almost flippantly about death.

"If I should die because of my racing, at least my parents and close friends will know that I went out with a smile on my face.

"I think of myself as a lion tamer. With all that horsepower, you try to utitilize as much of it as possible without getting hurt. There's a fine line between control of the car and complete disaster. That's what makes it so challenging."

Gabelich likes the feeling of fear.

"Many drivers express fear in different ways. My moment of fear comes just before the run. But when I climb into the car it's exhilarating—the adrenalin starts pumping. You think clear, you're in a world of your own. It's just out of sight."

Speed has also brought visions of death. Arfons and Breedlove survived their premonitions of impending doom. Donald Campbell did not. Campbell twice saw the messenger of death.

"When I took Bluebird out to Bonneville in 1960 I was convinced that I was going to kill myself. I had a presentiment of death when I was on vacation in Majorca just before I started the trip. It's the one time in my life I've had it, and sure enough everything went wrong from then on."

Less than 48 hours before he died in 1967, Campbell drew the Ace and Queen of Spades during a card game. For the fantastically superstitious Englishman, it was a forecast of death.

Campbell looked crestfallen. "Mary Queen of Scots turned up the same combination and knew

Vic Wilson, who drove the "Courage of Australia" dragster. (He will drive land-speed car). *Courtesy Mirror Newspapers Limited, Sydney, Australia.*

she would be beheaded. I know that one of my family is going to get the chop. I pray to God it isn't me."

The new playing cards were green-backed, the color Campbell believed was unlucky for him. Later that same night, he told a close friend, "Well, I reckon it should be over tomorrow—one way or the other."

The premonition came true as the jet-powered "Bluebird" soared off the surface of Lake Coniston in England at a speed of more than 300. The man who had set seven water and one land speed record disappeared into the pages of history.

Breedlove had an uneasy feeling the day before he wrecked his "Spirit of America" during the return run that cemented a 526 record in 1964.

"I had a feeling that I was going to get killed. I couldn't sleep that night. I was nervous on my first run, but I really hit it on the return. I could have gone 600 instead of 539.

"I lost the steering before I hit the mile. The "Spirit" drifted to the right. I came off the power

to straighten it out, and then I opened it up again at the far end of the mile.''

Trying to stop, Breedlove pressed the cockpit button to release a small pilot chute. ''I felt it come out and tear off the car. I hit the wheel brakes, but nothing happened.

''I heard myself saying 'let it slow down, slow down.' I wanted to throw ''Spirit'' into a spin, but without steering there was no way.

''I saw a telephone pole coming right at me. God must have moved it (the rear axle topped the pole, the wheel missing by inches). I saw this big pile of mud, hit it, flew about 35 feet into the air and down into the water. I knew I was going to die.''

But somehow Breedlove managed to release the canopy and swim to safety.

A kind of jubilant hysteria seized him.

''Do I qualify for the hydro-speed record, too?'' he asked. He embraced his father, Norman, and blurted, ''Dad, I bent my machine. Look.''

Beyond them only ''Spirit's tail was visible. The rest was submerged.

Breedlove had to be coaxed into the ambulance. At Wendover it took him 30 minutes to convince the doctors he was okay.

One year later, Craig had another brush with death. This time at 600 miles an hour. The ''Spirit of America-Sonic I'' veered to the right, off course. Breedlove twisted the steering wheel but nothing happened. He opened his braking chute but it yanked off.

The racer careened off the official timing area,

off the track, across wet salt, through an opening in a line of telephone poles and finally rolled to a stop in front of a salt water pond—nine miles from where he left the track.

The Los Angeles driver thanked his disc brakes for preventing a bath. Except for apparent slight collapsing of a rear body panel, the race car did not appear badly damaged. No tires blew out despite the pounding on the ungraded, soft surface of the off-track salt.

Arfons remembers his premonition. So does his wife, June.

''About a month before I left for the Flats, I had a dream. Did you ever have something happen to you and you think 'I've been here before,' and it was a dream you had a long time ago?

''When the car flipped the first time (November 17, 1966), I didn't know it was gone. It got up and was coming in to crash the second time and I knew I had been there before. I had this dream that I crashed at high speed.

''I was uneasy about the whole deal. The dream was on the back of my mind and I couldn't back out. I thought it was silly to be scared out of a chance to regain my record because of a dream.''

Adds June Arfons: ''I could tell something was wrong before he left for Utah. Art was fixing everything around the house. When Art finally told me he had a dream about the car crashing, I asked him to stay home.''

The dream almost turned out to be a nightmare.

6
Nature's Super-Highway

There are few places in the world where men can drive a four-wheeled missile faster than a speeding bullet.

With but one exception, all land speed attempts since the mid-1930s have taken place at the desolate Bonneville Salt Flats in Western Utah—3000 square miles and 500 million tons of salt.

The late Donald Campbell of England steered his "Bluebird" across lake Eyre in Australia to a wheel-driven record of 403.1 in 1964.

Popularity came to Bonneville when Campbell's legendary father, Sir Malcolm, sought a faster, safer and longer speedway than the sands of Ormond Beach in Florida. The strain of a car streaking across the sands at speeds approaching 300 miles an hour forced the crust to crack and thus ended a golden era of racing.

In 1935, Campbell took his "Bluebird" to Bonneville and became the first man to reach 300. His two-way average across the glistening flats: 301.13.

Thirty years later, Craig Breedlove shattered the 600 barrier in his jet-thrust "Spirit of America-Sonic I."

The Flats were named for Capt. Benjamin L.E. Bonneville, a French-born officer in the U.S. Army who explored the Rocky Mountain region during 1832-1836. Whether or not he actually touched what is now called the Bonneville Speedway isn't known.

Some historians credit a young scout by the name of Jedediah Smith and his party with being the first white people to touch their boots on the salt desert. Smith established trapping quarters on Bear River, and it was while returning there from a trip to California in 1827 that it is said he crossed the wasteland.

Later, in 1845, famed frontier scout "Kit" Carson and three others, acting as the vanguard for Colonel John Charles Fremont, explored western regions for the federal government. Fremont lost about 15 horses and mules in crossing the flats. Some writers contend that Carson was the first to actually cross what is now the Bonneville Speedway.

The following year Lansford W. Hastings, a young frontiersman, mapped an eastward course which cut through the salt. The ill-fated Donner Party battled across the salt in the fall of 1846. Their wagons sank through the salt where the crust was thin. They were forced to leave some of their belongings and their delay in crossing made them late in reaching the high Sierras. Snow overtook them. Some froze to death; others died of hunger. Only 44 of the original company of 87 reached their destination alive.

It wasn't until 1896, the same year that Utah became a state, that the potential of the flats for racing was discovered. That's when W.D. Rishel accidentally came to the salt.

William Randolph Hearst, the publisher, had just opened a newspaper in New York City and thought it would be a great publicity stunt to send a message by bicycle. The message would be sent by bicycle from Hearst's San Francisco Examiner to his New York Journal.

Rishel, then living in Cheyenne, Wyoming, received the assignment to blaze a bicycle trail from that town to Truckee, California.

Fighting thirst, sticky marshes and sweeping

clouds of mosquitos, Rishel crossed the Flats in 22 hours. Four years later, Rishel had the honor of driving the first car across the saline highway. The big Packard pushed the speedometer to 50 miles an hour.

In 1912, Rishel took A.L. Westgard, national pathfinder for the National Trails Association, out to the beds. Westgard agreed the Flats were the "greatest speedway on earth." Though a well-known automobile figure, Westgard's statement drew no excitement.

Air Force Missile Development Center, Holloman AFB, N.M. The 35,000-foot high-speed test track, from the south breech looking north, is maintained and operated by the Directorate of Test Track Facility, Air Force Missile Development Center, Holloman AFB, N.M. *Courtesy USAF.*

Bonneville was forgotten until 1914 when a barnstroming fleet of nine racing machines were brought into Salt Lake City. Rishel and other local business men arranged for an exhibition race on the salt. One hundred fifty-two tickets were sold for the event. Teddy Tezliff, driving the famed "Blitzen Benz" which Barney Oldfield had previously piloted to numerous speed records, clocked a torrid 141.73. His mile run lasted 25 2/5 seconds.

Years later, Rishel vivedly recalled the race.

"There was no electric timing device, so a good portion of the spectators brought stop-watches. A man with a flag was placed at each end of the measured mile, and we put the official timers in the middle so they could see both flags, which were waved as the "Blitzen Benz" roared by.

"When the race was finished, the timers announced that world record (25 3/5 seconds) had been bettered. Both the American Automobile Association and Automobile Club of America gave the record a chill shoulder."

Again the flats faded into racing oblivion, until a young carpenter from Salt Lake City by the name of Ab Jenkins came along. Jenkins first saw the salt in 1910 when he drove his motorcycle to a speed of 60 miles an hour. He made his second visit on a motorcycle shortly before World War I.

"This time I drove a motorcycle with much more 'vinegar' in its system," he wrote years later. "I soon found myself bucking a strong wind, the force of which would not permit me to sit up in the saddle of the machine, and so I grabbed a firm grip on the two handles and spread my body straight out, as though driving a child's snow sled. I stiffened my legs and gave her the works—50—60—70—80.

"That was traveling, and the ride gave my spinal

Air Force Missile Development Center, Holloman AFB, New Mexico. The 35,588-foot High Speed Test Track. The view was taken from the south breech looking north. The track is located in the Tularosa Basin of southern New Mexico. It is situated on the eastern edge of the White Sands Missile Range. Long periods of acceleration are possible with the present track with sufficient track length remaining to allow low G recovery of the system. The track can be readily extended should longer acceleration periods be required in the future.

cord more chills than any run I ever made on the salt flats.''

However, it wasn't until 1925 that Jenkins brought worldwide attention to the saline speedway. His race against a train and subsequent 24-hour marathon against the clock would bring the likes of Cobb, Campbell and Eyston to Utah. For years, Rishel campaigned to bring a highway across the Bonneville Salt Flats. In 1925, the highway was completed. As an added attraction to the planned celebration, Rishel asked his old friend if he would race the special excursion train from Salt Lake City to Wendover, a distance of 125 miles.

Ab Jenkins said he would—provided there was $250 riding on the outcome. The money was quickly raised and the race was on.

Streaking across the Flats, Ab beat the train by

five minutes. That run convinced him of the tremendous possibilities of the beds for racing.

Between 1926 and 1931 Jenkins kept busy, not only setting cross-country marks but American hill-climb records as well. During those years he never forgot his memorable race against a train.

In 1932, Jenkins returned to Utah for his first official races, peeled off the fenders of his Pierce-Arrow, and the 24-hour marathon began.

Pierce-Arrow officials laughed before the race when Jenkins told them he was going to drive his ''Mormon Meteor'' 2400 miles in 24 hours. Instead, he clocked 2710 miles. However, the 1932 run never became official because it was not timed by the AAA.

In mid-summer of 1933 he returned for an official 24-hour run. This time the achievement went into the record books—3000 miles in 25 hours, 30

This is a test of the T-38 aircraft escape system. In the test, a dummy is fired through the closed canopy, causing it to shatter. *Courtesy USAF.*

Athol Graham, Salt Lake City, Utah garage owner, takes a long look down the Bonneville Salt Flats as he kneels beside his $2,500 Allison-powered speed machine. *Courtesy Firestone Tire & Rubber Company.*

minutes and 36.62 seconds. The average speed: 117.77.

Seven years later Jenkins shattered all world's circular track records from one mile to 3868.14 miles, the number covered in 24 hours.

While his 12 cylinder, 750-horsepower "Mormon Meteor III" had a speed potential of 275 miles an hour, Jenkins was never interested in the world land-speed record. He left that to daredevils such as Campbell, Eyston and Cobb.

Born in 1883, Jenkins died in 1956 at the age of 73. His last assault upon his own records in 1951 failed because of car trouble. Jenkins was then 68 years old. Some of his numerous records included:

Year	Distance or Time	MPH
1936	48 hours	148.63
1950	24 hours	161.184
1950	1 hour	190.68
1940	1000 miles	172.804
1940	500 miles	177.229
1950	200 miles	190.92
1951	100 miles	190.657

Sir Malcolm Campbell, who had reached 276 at Ormond Beach in Florida, was determined to shatter the "300" barrier. In searching for a longer and smoother track, he arrived at the Flats in 1935. On September 3, he sped to a new two-way record of 301.13. After the run, which cemented the record, he called the Bonneville Salt Flats "The speed laboratory of the future."

Here's how it all began:

During the last stages of the ice age, some 70,000 to 100,000 years ago, when Utah's climate was damp and chilled and small glaciers flowed down the highest peaks, there was enough rain to form a huge lake. Lake Bonneville, a lake as big as Lake Michigan, covered western Utah from Salt Lake City to Wendover. This lake was 100 miles wide and nearly twice as long. The Great Salt Lake forms the edges of this vast lake.

To appreciate this lake fully, remember that both Wendover and Salt Lake City—125 miles apart on opposite shores—rest upon their old bed. The water reached a depth of 1000 feet over both towns.

As the huge lake, without an outlet, continued to receive the water from the streams and huge quantities of water evaporated from its surface, the water turned brackish.

The lake dried up. More water evaporated than flowed in, and the water, still containing all the mineral salt, became more and more salty.

Today, the Great Salt Lake is 25 percent salts (table salts, Epsom salts, and other kinds), so salty it is almost greasy to the touch and so dense a human body will not sink in it.

Thus, that salt was formed by entirely natural processes over a long period of time. The salt flats and the entire salt desert near Wendover are solid crystalline salts left on the ground when the western part of the huge lake basin dried up.

These Bonneville Salt Flats are not the only surface salt deposits, but are unique in their size—3,000 square miles or 35 percent larger than the state of Delaware.

7
A Rocket Is Poised

More than 40 years ago, German inventor-sportsman Fritz von Opel fired his rocket car for the first time. The date: May 24, 1928.

It was a thrilling sight for those who lined the Avus Speedway in Berlin. A newspaper report detailed the event: "The car started with a terrific roar emitting a sheet of flame and a cloud of yellow smoke as the rockets exploded. The machine gained momentum as one rocket after another, all of uniform power, were shot off—the car taking a lunge forward every time one exploded."

Estimated speed was 100 miles per hour for the driverless motor car, which attained an unheard-of speed of 420 miles per hour for a few seconds. The car was propelled by 12 rockets.

Von Opel felt there was practically no limit to the speed that could be reached by his rocket racer. However, the brilliant inventor never pursued the world land speed record. He would have easily outsped his rivals who were barely creeping into the 200 mile per hour zone.

It wasn't until 1965 that a rocket-powered car took dead aim on the land speed record. However, Walt Arfons' "Wingfoot Express," propelled by 25 rockets and driven by Bob Tatree, lacked the sustained thrust to shatter the record.

Despite the failure, the rocket era had been launched.

Five years later, another rocket car attempted to succeed where "Wingfoot Express" had failed. "The Blue Flame" was the five-year culmination of dreams, sweat and tears by Reaction Dynamics, Inc., of Milwaukee, Wiscosin.

The dream started with Ray Dausman, a young research technician who wasn't impressed by the speeds attained by conventional nitro-burning dragsters. They were clocking 205 in 7.5 seconds. Dausman was thinking in faster terms and discussed the situation with Dick Keller, a co-worker at the Chicage-based Illinois Institute of Technology Research Center. Keller felt the answer was a small, rocket-powered dragster.

The pair then devised a three-step program to build:

—A small prototype rocket motor to demonstrate their ability to design and construct such a powerplant.

—A prototype rocket-propelled dragster with a larger rocket engine, and finally,

—A land speed vehicle with a still larger rocket engine.

As they planned, Art Arfons was capturing headlines with his jet-powered "Green Monster," that set a new speed record of 536.75.

Keller and Dausman, meanwhile, tested their first 25-pound thrust engine with hydrogen peroxide in the fall of 1964. Their testing "instruments" included a home movie camera and a bathroom scale.

Their first rocket engine performed to specification.

Keller and Dausman advanced to step 2, with the help of Pete Farnsworth, a professional driver and car builder.

The three formed a partnership—Reaction Dynamics—and with their own funds began building the prototype rocket-engined dragster, X-1. It's 2,500-pound thrust motor was completed in April, 1965.

That fall found the "jet set" back at Bonneville

Gary Gabelich after record run. *Courtesy American Gas Association.*

as Craig Breedlove and his "Spirit of America-Sonic I" outdueled the Arfons brothers. Breedlove sent the record soaring to 600.601.

The X-1 chassis was completed in the spring of 1966. That summer, Keller became the first person to test drive X-1. Two seconds of rocket power sent him coasting to the end of the track. It also sent him searching for a professional driver for future high-speed tests.

Keller and Farnsworth turned to an old friend, Chuck Suba of Calumet City, Illinois. Suba, a veteran dragracer with jet experience, agreed to drive the X-1 with the understanding that he would get first crack at piloting their land speed car.

In September of 1966, Suba drove the X-1, minus the body, to a speed of 203.39 miles an hour in a high-speed test run. Body work was completed in April 1967, with Farnsworth doing the fabricating himself.

Testing continued that summer and changes were made until fall. At that time the X-1 was to take on the jet dragsters, who refused to race unless they were given time handicaps. These were given and the holiday's climax came after

Suba granted Walt Arfons' "Green Monster" dragster a half-second handicap.

The "Monster's" afterburner belched, sounding the cue for the roar of the rocket. Suba streaked past the "Green Monster," and the finish line, in 6.32 seconds for the quarter mile.

The fall of 1967 found Keller calculating motor performance possibilities for a land speed record contender. He and Dausman concluded that the power of a rocket engine using hydrogen peroxide could be almost doubled by adding a fuel.

Keller's employers, the Institute of Gas Technology, were then studying uses of liquefied natural gas fuel in their labs. Its performance potential seemed like a "natural" for the car and for the natural gas industry.

Reaction Dynamics conferred with Northern Illinois Gas Company in January of 1968. The Illinois firm agreed to pursue the proposal further with the natural gas industry and its trade organization, the American Gas Association.

Spring found X-1 with a larger fuel tank and faster elapsed times. Some weight was removed and by September the rocket dragster was hitting speeds in the high 200s.

Racing against the clock, Suba turned in a blistering 265.48 run which lasted just 5.90 seconds at an Oklahoma City strip.

That run proved important because among the spectators that damp Sunday afternoon were

Gary Gabelich, following his serious drag strip accident. *Courtesy Rocket Man Productions.*

Gary Gabelich in drag boat. *Courtesy Rocket Man Productions.*

natural gas industry officials who enthusiastically gave the land speed project the green light.

Less than a month later personal tragedy struck the project. On September 13, 1968, Chuck Suba died behind the wheel of a piston-engine dragster he was testing for a friend.

The search for a driver would end with the selection of Gary Gabelich.

The gas industry decided to go into the land speed business to demonstrate the safety and versatility of liqufied natural gas (LNG) as a potential fuel in automobiles and aircraft.

A total of 30 natural gas companies in the United States and Canada became chief sponsors in the $500,000 venture. Specialists in rocket engine de-

sign and aerospace engineering joined the team as consultants.

Goodyear agreed to build the tires, tested on the company's multi-stage dynamometer at more than 700 miles an hour.

Construction of "The Blue Flame" began in early 1969, after wind-tunnel tests conducted at Ohio State University indicated that its pencil-shaped design would permit the vehicle to travel at speeds in excess of 900 miles per hour. In other words, the car was stable. Stability means that aerodynamic forces tend to keep the car moving in a straight line and direct it back into a correct, safe course in the event of an unexpected occurence. The wind tunnel tests also showed the rocket car

The X-1, a rocket-engine dragster which Reaction Dynamics, Inc., built to demonstrate their ability to design and construct the "Blue Flame" land speed record vehicle. The X-1 delivered 2,500 lb. thrust. The "Blue Flame" delivered 13,000. *Courtesy Hot Rod.*

would not lift off the ground—a "must" for safe operation.

Pressure forces developed by high speeds were uniform and lower than expected, indicating that the car's design structure would withstand high velocity loads.

Completed in the summer of 1970, "The Blue Flame" was 37 feet, 4.6 inches long. The designers originally planned to have only one front wheel, but then the car would technically have been classified as a three-wheeler or motorcycle. So they built two front wheels only one inch apart. The rocket engine, stored in spheres in the car's needle nose, was placed behind the driver. The body and chassis were built as one integral unit with a lightweight aluminum skin covering the semi-monocoque chassis. The front wheels were locked in such a way that the steering wheel could be turned only one degree. In addition, a rudder just behind the cockpit was installed to help keep the 5,500-pound car on line.

Other dimensions: width (overall), 7 feet, 8 inches; height (top of cockpit), 5 feet, 1.5 inches; height (top of tail fin), 8 feet, 8 inches; wheelbase, 306.1 inches.

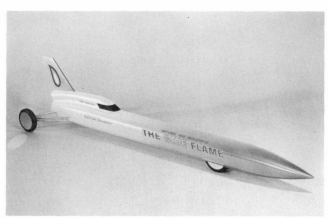

Scale model of "Blue Flame." *Courtesy Institute of Gas Technology.*

Among the numerous consultants who assisted in the design of the "Blue Flame" are (left to right) Harshad Parikh. Prahlad Thakur, Dr. Paul Torda, Manoj Adhikari, Tom Morel, Dr. Sarunas Uzgiris, and Krishna Pandey, all of IIT's Mechanical and Aerospace Engineering Department. *Courtesy Illinois Institute of Technology.*

Dick Keller, manager of project development for Reaction Dynamics, holding the 1/25-scale supersonic wind tunnel test model of "Blue Flame." The model tests indicate that the rear wheel fairings should be removed to reduce supersonic drag and improve stability. *Courtesy American Gas Association.*

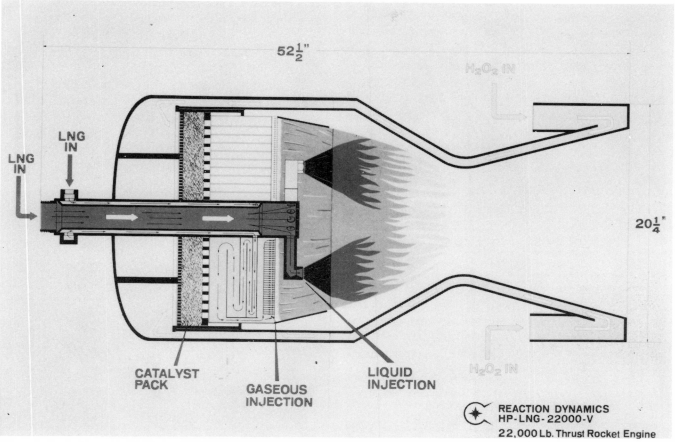

52½"

H₂O₂ IN

LNG IN

LNG IN

20¼"

H₂O₂ IN

CATALYST PACK

GASEOUS INJECTION

LIQUID INJECTION

REACTION DYNAMICS
HP-LNG-22000-V
22,000 Lb. Thrust Rocket Engine

Reaction Dynamics' LNG-fueled rocket motor, used to propel "Blue Flame." The principle of operation is fairly uncomplicated, as illustrated above. Hydrogen peroxide (H_2O_2) is circulated through the outer cooling jacket before being decomposed over the catalyst pack. The products of decompositions, super-heated steam (H_2O) and gaseous oxygen (O_2), flow over a finned heat exchanger, converting 25% of the LNG to a hot (above the flash point) gas. Thermal ignition occurs at the point of gaseous injection of the LNG into the hot oxygen stream. This primary combustion further raises the temperature to the point where the remaining 75% of the LNG can be injected as a liquid to react with the remaining oxygen from the H_2O_2 decomposition. *Courtesy American Gas Association.*

Ray Dausman, of Reaction Dynamics, examining the heat exchanger section of the motor of "Blue Flame." *Courtesy American Gas Association.*

"The Blue Flame" was built to accelerate from zero to 750 miles per hour in just 7.5 seconds. While the car's rocket engine was designed to deliver 22,000 pounds of thrust—58,000 horsepower—it was modified for 13,000 pounds of thrust.

Riveted construction was used in the monocoque portion of "Blue Flame." A .040-inch thick aluminum skin was riveted to the fabricated framework. The skin was fully stressed in that area, contributing to the rigidity of the vehicle. This type of construction allowed the maximum usable internal volume with minimum weight and external volume. *Courtesy American Gas Association.*

"This car is capable of tremendous speed," commented Ray Dausman. "But we'll settle for 607 miles an hour this year, just enough to break Craig Breedlove's record. Then we'll set our sights on the sound barrier and after that, we'll shoot for 1000 miles an hour."

The car underwent static firing tests in July of 1970. This marked the first time that Gabelich squeezed into the cockpit.

"We chained the car to a 12-foot pole and turned the engine on. The engine developed about 12,000 pounds of thrust—equivalent to about 630 miles an hour—and it felt real good. It was more like hold-

Assembly of the central monocoque span of "Blue Flame's" fuselage is upside-down here, with the front wheel compartment in the foreground. In the background is the X-1 rocket-powered dragster, which was used to demonstrate the feasibility of rocket propulsion in a racing car. *Courtesy American Gas Association.*

ing back a horse that wanted to go," he commented.

Liquefied natural gas and hydrogen peroxide provided the enormous amount of thrust. LNG, the liquid form of natural gas chilled to minus 258 degrees Fahrenheit, served as the fuel and hydrogen peroxide as the oxidizing agent which cooled the engine to prevent overheating.

In operation, "The Blue Flame" engine was designed to permit natural gas to be used as a liquid, gas, or both.

Here's how it worked:

Combustion starts in two stages. First, the ox-

The central monocoque span of "Blue Flame" is 20 feet long. Extruded aluminum H-beams and welded rings form a substructure to which the .040 inch thick fully-stressed aluminum skin is riveted. Hatch covers over the propellent tank and front wheel compartments are also stressed when bolted into position. The entire structure is held in alignment on a steel I-beam while being fabricated. The tubular structure at the rear of the chassis will house propellent control valves and Reaction Dynamics' 22,000-pound thrust LNG-fueled rocket engine. *Courtesy American Gas Association.*

idizer flow is established. Hydrogen peroxide goes through a catalyst pack which converts it from a liquid to a super-heated gas of 1,400 degrees.

Then LNG enters a heat exchanger where it vaporizes and is brought to combustion temperature. The gas is injected to the combustion chamber with the oxygen provided by the hydrogen peroxide. A stable flame front is established and the remaining LNG injected to bring the engine to full power.

Hydrogen peroxide alone gives the engine a thrust up to 12,000 pounds. But when LNG is fed into the hot gas, the raction almost doubles the thrust.

Engine thrust varies by controlling the flow rates of the propellents with a foot-controled throttle.

As in any project of this sort, there was a risk factor involved. However, Pete Farnsworth felt the risks had been reduced to the bare minimum. Take the matter of tires, for instance.

"The tread surface is smooth and extremely thin to help prevent heat buildup. All tires have high-strength steel wire inside, so they can be

Ray Dausman compares the original 25-pound thrust prototype rocket motor in his hand with the 22,000-pound thrust LNG-fueled rocket motor used in "Blue Flame." *Courtesy American Gas Association.*

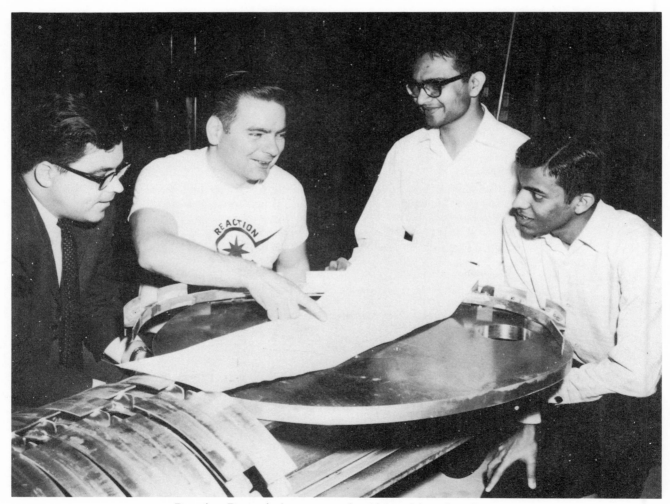

Reaction Dynamics' manager of vehicle engineering, Pete Farnsworth (2nd from left), discussing "Blue Flame's" design with structural engineering consultants, (from left) Dr. S. Carl Uzgiris, Shashi Kurani, and Monoj Adhikari, all of Illinois Institute of Technology. The semi-monocoque design was thoroughly analyzed, before construction began, using an analog computer to simulate dynamic loads on the vehicle. *Courtesy American Gas Association.*

As the ''Blue Flame'' chassis nears completion, the slim, needle-like shape becomes apparent. Access is provided to the propulsion system components by removing the nose cone, the upper half of the center body span, or the rear tubular structures which envelope the engine and propellent control valves. Additional small access panels are located on the vehicle for replenishing the propellents and high-pressure nitrogen and helium gases between runs. *Courtesy American Gas Association.*

''Blue Flame'' crew. *Courtesy Institute of Gas Technology.*

(Left to right) Pete Farnsworth, Dick Keller, Gary Gabelich, Dean Dietrich. *Courtesy Goodyear Tire and Rubber Company.*

inflated to 250 pounds per square inch. That will also reduce heat and friction.

"If a tire does blow, the car would swerve out of control and possibly break up. The driver's capsule is of heavier aluminum than the rest of the car, so we hope he would be protected.

"We considered an ejection seat. But if "Blue Flame" tumbles, the driver could be blown into the ground. Even if the car stays upright, he would have to be shot 500 feet into the air before the chute could open."

What would happen if a fire started on board?

"An aircraft-type extinguishing system has been installed. It will sense the heat waves and instantly spray the car interior with foam."

The driver would wear a fire suit and an oxygen mask.

What if the parachutes don't work?

"There's a complete backup system. If both systems fail, "Blue Flame" will shoot across six miles of salt flats and end up in the Great Salt Lake."

Gary Gabelich was anxious for a crack at the land speed title.

"I feel like a kid on Christmas Eve. I can hardly wait until we get to Bonneville. I have complete confidence in the gentlemen from Reaction Dynamics.

"Over five years of research in the fields of aeronautics, rocketry, metallurgy and tire design went into the project prior to construction. They have invested a lot of time, money and patience... and they wouldn't put me in there if they felt they were going to hurt me."

"Blue Flame"—start of a record run. *Courtesy Goodyear Tire and Rubber Company.*

"Blue Flame" completes a day of trial runs at the Bonneville
Salt Flats. *Courtesy Institute of Gas Technology.*

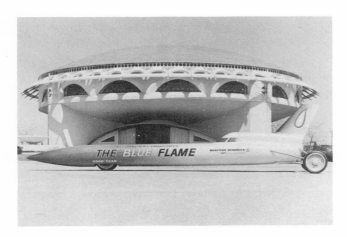

"Blue Flame" at Houston Astrodome. *Courtesy American
Gas Association.*

Gary Gabelich after 622.407 record. *Courtesy Goodyear Tire and Rubber Company.*

8
Gary Gabelich—A Dream Comes True

As a youngster growing up in San Pedro, California, Gary Gabelich dreamed of driving cars faster than anyone else.

"I'd spend hours drawing cars, like in the Buck Rogers comic strip," he recalls. But how many get the chance to turn daydreams into reality?

On October 23, 1970, Gary Gabelich became the fastest man on wheels when he drove the rocket-powered "Blue Flame" to a new world land speed record of 622.407 at the Bonneville Salt Flats.

Now he dreams of going faster—faster than the speed of sound. It would add another exciting chapter to his thrill-a-minute life.

The lean, handsome six-footer is a 20th century adventurer. Gary has been a test astronaut, piloted a 1,200-horsepower fuel-burning hydroplane to a quarter-mile record of 200.44, and made 59 parachute jumps—including several over 30,000 feet.

Gabelich was born August 29, 1940 in San Pedro. His first taste of speed came at 17.

"I knew several guys who had an old coupe, and they let me help them. Since they were four or five years older, I guess you could say I was their donkey—doing all the dirty work.

"One day, out at the old Santa Ana strip, I had the chance to drive the car, but the strip manager said I was too young and needed written permission from my parents.

"I told him I'd be right back. I went to a gas station around the corner, signed my parents' names, and then ran 138 miles an hour—the fastest the car had ever turned."

In the next five years, Gabelich drove every exotic piece of racing equipment on the market, ranging from gas and fuel rails to jet dragsters.

He handled the jet car "Untouchable I," owned by Romeo Palamides, and later piloted another jet racer owned by Mickey Thompson and Art Malone.

In 1963, Gary achieved the dream of all drag racers, outdueling national champion Don Garlits in the first United Drag Racing Association meet.

As a boat driver, he was the National Drag Boat Association fuel hydro champion (1965). Three years later, he captured two other prestigious titles—American Powerboat Association nitro-fuel and National Drag Boat Association's gasoline hydroplane championships.

By clocking 200.44 in 1969 in "Crisis", a hydro powered by a Chrysler hemi-engine, Gabelich topped Tommy Fultz's quarter-mile record for prop-driven boats.

As if his racing activities didn't provide enough excitement, Gary took up skydiving. "I tried unsuccessfully to sell my skydiving and drag racing as a package," he recalls with a wry smile.

"I had the brilliant idea of parachuting down to a drag strip, unbuckling my gear, then driving my funny car. But the strip managers didn't go for it. They were afraid I would impale myself on telephone wires or land in the crowd."

For a man who drove a $500,000 car faster than any man, Gabelich began his career rather modestly as a $1.29 an hour mailboy for North American Rockwell. That was in 1959.

After holding that job, and then a variety of others, he passed a battery of physical and mental tests and in 1962 was selected as one of seven test astronauts to work in the company's program of environmental control studies for NASA's Apollo project.

Part of the program called for living in space capsules for up to 12 days under simulated high-altitude, re-entry and zero gravity conditions.

As a test astronaut, he also jumped from high altitudes with cameras to record the action of parachutes used in the re-entry of outer-space capsules.

When it finally came time to decide between racing and a space career, Gary Gabelich didn't hesitate one bit. "It would be groovy and exciting to go to the moon," he said, "but I like racing too much to give it up for that."

While Gabelich was blasting out a reputation on the west coast, plans were already underway in Milwaukee, Wisconsin to build a rocket-propelled land speed car.

Many of the top names in high-speed racing were considered, including Craig Breedlove and Art Arfons, who had combined to set eight unlimited land speed records.

But a hot-rodder from Long Beach, California was selected.

"Even before I signed to drive it," recalls Gabelich, "I discussed it and studied it with several engineers. The wind tunnel tests, although not conclusive, showed that the car was stable and the construction sound.

"We preferred to go rocket, rather than jet. A rocket engine develops more power than any other engine. Its weight is the lowest for each pound of thrust it produces."

Gary had complete confidence in the designers and builders, Reaction Dynamics. "They've invested a lot of time, money and patience and they wouldn't put me in there if they felt they were going to hurt me."

One of the reasons Gary Gabelich was selected was because of his coolness under fire. Despite several crashes, he had never lost control of his car. Like the time he was driving his $12,000 funny car when it blew up and almost melted his flame suit. "It was the last run of the night for all the money, $1,000 in cash. Just as I approached the last timing light, the engine blew.

"The oil leaked down and hit the headers (exhaust pipes). The oil ignited and burned a hole in the firewall, which separates the engine compartment from the cockpit.

"We hit 180 on that run but before I knew it the flames were in the cockpit. My pants caught on fire and they worked their way up to my jacket.

"I was in the car for eight or nine seconds but instinctively pulled the parachute to slow the car down. The heat got so intense it actually broke the lens of my goggles and burned the chute off.

"I jumped out of the car before it came to a stop—the heat was so unbearable. I just got on the top of the car, bailed out and rolled in the dirt. After I got out, I threw dirt on the car to put the fire out, which now that I think of it was pretty ridiculous."

The car was a total loss. Fortunately, Gary escaped unharmed.

It was love at first sight for Gabelich and the 6500-pound rocket racer. He knew he had a winner when he fired up "Blue Flame" during static tests in July of 1970.

"We chained her to a post sunk 12 feet in the ground and turned the engine on. She felt real good. It was like holding her back when she really wanted to go." Instruments rigged to the car showed the speed estimated at 700 miles an hour—more than enough to capture the land-speed record.

As the time drew closer to run at Bonneville, Gary became more and more anxious. "People think I'm crazy to do this, but I've prepared myself mentally. As the days pass, I feel like a kid waiting for Christmas morning. I want to drive her. I want to drive her real bad."

He got his wish in September of 1970.

On September 13, the California hot-rodder looked over the desolate Salt Flats.

"I walked part of the course and drove my rental car back and forth over most of the track. The surface was hard, perfect for racing." At least, for the time being.

He would take his first ride four days later after the wheel bearings had been replaced, some minor parachute problems solved, and after the arrival of fuel.

Neither Gabelich nor his sponsors planned to attack the record head-on. Speeds would be steadily increased until all was ready for full-throttle runs.

"I can tell you one thing," he said. "I'm not going out there with a Banzai attitude. No kamikaze runs for me. As much as I want the record, I want to be around to enjoy it."

On September 17, Gabelich clocked a leisurely 185 in his first run. But during that ride, an engine backfire caused a mild explosion.

"We injected the fuel into a chamber at too low a temperature," explained project manager Dean Dietrich of the Institute of Gas Technology. "That caused the explosion, which doesn't appear to have damaged anything seriously."

But Dietrich was wrong in his early diagnosis.

The explosion bent the injector nozzles, which pumped liquified natural gas and hydrogen peroxide into the combustion chamber of the engine. In addition, several seams on the stainless steel engine had to be rewelded after minute flaws were discovered.

Three days later—September 20—Gabelich was clocked at 411.23. "It was a perfect run. This is the fastest I've ever traveled on land. It felt good. It was out of sight."

While the "Blue Flame" was recording speeds in the 400 mile-an-hour range, for some reason the car was developing only 11,000 of its 22,000 pounds of potential thrust.

"We're just not getting the thrust out of the engine," moaned Gabelich after a 450 mph sortie. "Sure I'm disappointed, but we haven't given up. After we had the first malfunction of the engine, she never did run up to specification.

"That's why we're taking a break to regroup, you might say. When we come back we'll be ready for an attempt at the record. But right now all I can do is thank the crew for such a fine job of working with the car."

The team broke up on September 25 to await the arrival of a new catalyst pack from Buffalo, New York. Back on the salt two weeks later, "Blue Flame" hit 462 and 478 burning only hydrogen peroxide.

"We were practically out of LNG and we wanted to be very gingerly with the new catalyst pack," said Dietrich. The runs, however, were not without incident.

Midway through the first solo, Gabelich popped his safety chutes prematurely. As it turned out, it was a necessary maneuver, for he became separated from his oxygen mask and was forced to hold the oxygen line to the face mask with one hand and steer the car with the other.

"Hell, I couldn't breathe," Gabelich exclaimed. "But I didn't panic." Then he added: "Wasn't it a pretty run? She'll go. I know it. She'll really roar when we put in the LNG."

Forty-eight hours later another mishap occured. This time the safety chutes failed to open and Gary finally halted the runaway car four miles past the point he had intended to stop.

"I came close to pulling a Breedlove. If I had been going in the other direction like Craig did in 1964 I would have hit the highway and the power poles beyond that—and God knows what would have happened."

As it turned out, he stopped the car on slick, slushy salt some eight miles north of the USAC timing shack. It took the crew until 11 o'clock that night to pull "Blue Flame" out of the muddy bog.

"The biggest problem was with the support cars and spectators," Gary laughed. "The dozen cars and an ambulance needed tow trucks to get out of the mess. There we were, all of us stuck. It was almost like quicksand where I stopped. We had to get some jeeps and winches to pull us out."

Gary estimated the car was hitting 550 when he released the safety chutes, but nothing happened.

"Apparently enough radiant heat was coming off the exhaust systems to melt the nylon shield on the chutes," said co-builder Dick Keller. "The drogue guns fired, but with the nylon shields destroyed it was like firing a blank shell."

Gary Gabelich took the episode in stride.

"It won't be a problem once we build an aluminum shield to protect the nylon ropes from "The Flame's" exhaust. This is one of the reasons we keep running tests at higher and higher speeds. You don't know precisely what will happen until you do it."

Walking the long miles back to dry salt, Gabelich smiled and spoke simply and firmly. "We'll set the record before we leave the Flats."

The runaway took place on his fifth run of the day. Until then, "Blue Flame" had upped its speed from 477 to 562 miles an hour—just 40 under Breedlove's record of 600.601.

"We're getting a little excited," admitted Dean Dietrich. "If the run coming up is close to the record we'll go for it and get out of here."

Gary thought he had to try for it. "We want that record. The crew is getting a little tight and I'm getting a little flustered."

Enlarging the injectors would provide a circular motion for the LNG flow, thus allowing the fuel to burn longer and provide more power. But even with the enlarged injector, all the rocket car could manage was a disappointing 553.401.

"You've got to get me more horsepower," Gabelich barked. "She wants to go. Just bring on the power." One way was to continue experimenting with the fuel mixture in hopes of finding the right combination. The injector nozzles could be enlarged even more.

Use of a push car was also considered. USAC rules permitted a vehicle to be pushed in order to give it an extra boost before the engine was fired. Thus, some of the inertia could be overcome and power that had been wasted in getting the car rolling could be used for pure acceleration.

Under that plan, a truck approaching speeds of 70 miles an hour would push the 5,500-pound car before the driver backed off to allow Gabelich to fire-up the engine.

Gusting winds prevented any record attempts the next day, October 14, so Gary and his crew played a game of touch football. It was his way of relaxing after a frustrating month on the Flete.

Twenty-four hours later it was business as usual. The first order of the day was a two-second burst of the rocket engine to warm up the catalyst pack.

Then a truck pushed "Blue Flame" two miles before Gabelich kicked the rocket engine to life. Speed for the flying mile: 546.614. Two hours later the rocket racer clocked an even faster 581.021.

The stage had been set for an all-out assault.

At 5:35 p.m. (Rocky Mountain time), the 38-foot missile on wheels was poised 1½ miles from the timing lights. Seconds later it was a blur, a 160-pound man riding a smoking volcano.

And what a ride! Official speed was 609, the fastest man had traveled in land-speed history. How did it feel to go that fast?

"You're really pushed back hard in the seat and you can't pull yourself forward. You don't have time to think. You're locked in trying to keep her in line. You know you have to aim her between the lights. It's a beautiful feeling—all that horse-power."

Now it was a race against the clock to ready the car for the return run within 60 minutes. "Blue Flame" was pressurized and fully fueled when a seal in the regulator suddenly broke.

High-pressure hydrogen peroxide sprayed over the nose section of the racer and hit some of the crew members. There was a brief puff of smoke and fire which was quickly extinguished. Two crew members suffered face burns and were taken to a Salt Lake City hospital, 125 miles away.

By the time the excitement was over time had run out. The 609 run had been nullified. Part of the car was then torn down and a 39-cent tube of toothpaste used to fine-grind part of the handmade regulator. "Blue Flame" fired perfectly after the minor repairs.

Gary made back-to-back bursts of 604.027 and 599.300 for a blistering two-way average of 601.655. While it was faster than Breedlove's record, it still wasn't fast enough. The rule was specific—a record had to eclipsed by one percent—meaning Gabelich had to average 607 miles per hour.

"That's racing," was the dejected driver's comment when told by USAC officials that his record bid had failed. "I don't know what went wrong," Dietrich lamented. "I thought the run looked terrific. We'll work something out."

On the 599 run, the braking parachute malfunctioned and Gabelich careened off the track for 1½ miles before coming to a halt. The pilot chute deployed properly at 400, but the second stage or larger chute was released at too high a speed, forcing Gary to ride the rocket racer out with the smaller parachute. He left the end of the course at about 200 miles an hour. "Blue Flame" remained upright and the driver wasn't hurt.

Three days later—October 21—Gary Gabelich gunned the car to an even faster clocking of 621.624. A leaking regulator valve, however, prevented a return run. The valve regulated the amount of fuel pressure going into the hydrogen peroxide and LNG tanks.

"When it's not functioning you can't run really, Gary said, dejectedly. "You don't have the thrust. I know we can get more out of the car. We'll get the record when the fuel arrives. We'll put more heat into the engine—and more thrust."

A new regulator was built and a higher and more potent concentration of hydrogen peroxide ordered. It arrived on October 22, but gusting winds prevented any runs that day.

At that point, Gabelich had made 22 runs. A strong bond had developed between man and machine. "I love her. I've never driven a race car that handles so well. I feel like I'm having an affair with her. It's just unreal."

Seconds before the cockpit was sealed on Friday, October 23, Gary knelt by the needle-nose of the car. He carassed the nose and talked to it in a whisper.

"Let's do it together, baby. Give me a good

ride. Let's go, baby. You can do it. We can do it together, baby."

Now he was alone with his "baby". At 11:40 a.m., the former test astronaut adjusted his love beads and cradled his St. Christopher medal in his hands. In a split second the rocket car disappeared in a stream of white smoke as it streaked toward the target almost two miles away.

This time there were no problems as "Blue Flame" blasted through the measured mile in 5.89 seconds. Speed: 617.602. The the car was re-fueled, the safety chutes repacked. And again the 31-year-old driver knelt by the nose, rubbing it fondly, his lips moving.

"That was far out, baby, but we're not through yet. We've got to do it one more time and do it better. We can do it. Just you and me. We can do it. Now, let's go and do our thing together, you and me, baby, you and me."

With 12 minutes remaining in the countdown, "Blue Flame" flashed across the salt flats, ac-celerating through the mile in 5.739 seconds. The even faster 627.287 run cemented a new land speed record of 622.407.

"The mile markers went by real fast and the mountains just sat on the sidelines," bubbled a jubilant Gary Gabelich. "The air speed indicator was showing top speeds between 640 and 660 in the middle of the traps. It was a wild ride. We really got with it. I'm very happy.

"It was smooth, very smooth. It was just a little mushy at the end of the run, but that was probably due to the soft salt. The car handled like a dragster. She's a fantastic machine."

Dick Keller, co-builder of "Blue Flame," called it "a dream come true. It got out there just as quick as a fuel dragster. As far as handling, it was as good as we could have hoped. We never made one chassis adjustment the whole time we were out there."

"Terrific, terrific," raved project manager Dean Dietrich. "I really couldn't believe it. We had a good flame throughout the run and every-thing ran just perfectly. I'm glad it's over."

Even the usually dead-panned Joe Petrali, who supervised the seven-man USAC timing crew, was all smiles. "This is the smoothest-handling car I've ever seen. The suspension was built in such a way that there was no buffeting. The car just seemed to glide across the salt."

Moments later, Gary and his father, Mel Gabelich of Los Angeles, walked away from the crowd. Gary was smiling. Tears streamed down his father's face. They didn't seem to mind the pelting rain that was turning the salt into mush. Gary Gabelich had beaten the record and the weather.

What happens to a man after he sets the unli-mited land-speed record?

In Gary's case, it meant living out of a suitcase for 18 months, making public appearances throughout the United States and abroad.

He and "Blue Flame" not only apeared at auto shows, but the fastest man on wheels visited numerous junior high schools and high schools.

"The kids wanted to know what did it really feel like to go that fast. I tried to put them in the driver's seat. I tried to communicate to them what it felt like. A lot of them wanted to know what happened overseas.

"It was an open question type of thing. Some wanted to know what I thought about drugs, about this or that. It was a great experience and educa-tion."

Gabelich also made three USO tours, visiting servicemen in Japan, the Philippines, Okinawa, Hawaii and Vietnam. "It gave me a good feeling to go over there, talk with the guys and rap with them a little about home."

Gary became close to becoming a war zone casualty.

"They kept us away from the demilitarized zone in Vietnam, but we were pretty close. I saw a chopper get shot down, one that we were sup-posed to catch but missed.

"It was my fault. I was in a hooch with a bunch of guys, just rapping with them. Two people were killed and a couple others injured when the chop-per went down. I guess it could have been me."

When Gary Gabelich returned to the United States, he and his associates began building a four-wheel funny car.

"For one thing, it was the first four-wheel drive monocoque, rear-engine funny car. It was all handmade, even the wheels. It developed 1,500 to 2,000 horsepower, depending on how much nitro-methane you were running in the engine." Speed potential was 225-235 miles an hour.

"It was gonna be an exhibition car at first. Then we were gonna change bodies on it and run it as a dragster." Gabelich invested heavily in the ex-perimental dragster.

"The money that I made from making the record with "Blue Flame," the money I made from appearances, plus the money given to me by various sponsors all went into the car."

Gary Gabelich was in the early stages of testing the car. On April 7, 1972, his funny car smashed into a guard rail at Orange County International Raceway in Irvine, California, overturned, began disintegrating and burst into flames.

In the violent force of the crash, the car's rear end came off and wheels flew in all directions. Witnesses said the car rolled 200 feet.

"We were making long burnouts, that is smoking all four tires. I'd smoke the tires maybe 100 yards, then I'd smoke the tires an eighth of a mile.

"It happened real fast," recalls Gabelich. "I got down just about to the 1,000-foot mark when I found myself in a sideways drift—and then into the guard rail.

"When I hit the guard railing the front drive wheels came off, the car spun around and down the track without a front end, and went underneath the guard rail on the left side of the track.

"When it went underneath the railing, it took out five eight-by-eights. I was kinda wedged in the tub underneath the guard railing. Then the car flew back over the railing and back on the track and landed sideways, burning."

Gary Gabelich remained conscious during the crash.

"I tried to undo my seat belt and I couldn't get it undone with my left hand so I pulled down my goggles with my right hand. My left hand was laying down by where my left elbow is. It was hanging by a few tendons and some skin, like a wet dishrag.

"Then I realized my left leg wasn't where it was supposed to be. It was alongside of my body, kind of crumpled up in a weird way. I knew I was really messed up."

Part of the guard rail was tangled in Gary's leg, which was partially wrapped around the steering column.

"I was pulling some of the guard rail metal off me when the crew arrived. They put me in back of a station wagon and we made it to Tustin Community Hospital real fast."

Gabelich was on the operating table for six hours. Besides his hand injury, his heel was ripped off, his foot crushed. All told, he underwent six operations.

"At first the doctors told me I might be lucky to regain 65 percent use of my hand. But look," he said six months later, "I have more than that, probably 85 percent. Some of the nerve endings are gone and I've lost some of the feeling, but it's part of me, not a hook."

The leg was another matter.

"I have a steel pin or rod running into my heel. I almost lost the leg a couple of times when gangrene developed, but they were able to clear it up. It's bent all out of shape—mostly to the left—but that means I'll be able to run around left hand corners real fast."

Doctors predicted he wouldn't be well enough to resume racing for 18 months. "Maybe the accident was really a blessing in disguise. It's given me plenty of time to think about the sound barrier project, work up presentations to prospective sponsors. You don't raise $500,000 for such a venture overnight. Believe me, it's a lot easier going out and just driving a car."

Despite the serious accident, Gabelich felt confident all along that he would be able to resume his racing career.

"I want to live as much as the next guy, probably more so because I enjoy what I'm doing. But I'd be just a vegetable if I was forced to quit. You have to be a driver to understand what I'm talking about. Besides, I've paid my dues now.

"I've been injured about as badly as one man can and lived. I figure it can't happen twice."

9
Craig Breedlove—"The Spirit of America"

Nobody scoffs at Craig Breedlove anymore.

"There was a lot of ridicule when I started out," he recalls. "Breaking the land speed record sounds like a sort of way-out thing. A lot of people thought I'd never make it. There were times when I didn't think I would either."

Now, when he talks about smashing the sound barrier in a rocket racer—becoming the first to go 300 on water—bettering the wheel-driven record in the late Donald Campbell's "Bluebird"—the experts take Craig Breedlove seriously.

Some people only dream of conquering new frontiers. Men like Craig Breedlove turn dreams into reality.

"All I want to do is break the sound barrier. Then I'll get myself a dog and go run along the beach with him. I'll let somebody else break 1,000."

A moment later, however, he adds, "Of course, I couldn't very well quit on the job. I mean, if I went 760, say, and somebody else turned around and went 820—well—."

Why the world water record?

"I've set the world motorcycle record with the first "Spirit of America" and the land speed record with "Sonic I." I want the water speed mark, too."

Breedlove's "Aquamerica" is at the drawing board stage. It would cost $80,000 to $90,000 to bring it to life.

The boat would be 34 feet long with two jet engines up front to develop a total thrust of 6,000 pounds.

"I think she would be capable of 400, but I'd be happy with 300." Then he explains how the needle-thin craft would stay waterborne at 300. At this speed only three square inches of hull will touch the water, he points out. The 4,000-pound hydroplane will be delicately balanced on its two forward sponsons (pontoons) and the bottom of the tail.

"Two General Electric CJ610 jet engines with 3,000 pounds of thrust each will be mounted atop the sponsons. Their location in front of the cockpit puts the center of gravity far forward, giving the Aquamerica the same aerodynamic stability as a dart or arrow.

"The hydroplane can't flip at high speed because it's vertically and horizontally stabilized by the engine location, tail design and a ground-effect air foil."

The foil, which he describes as an upside-down airplane wing, will cause the boat to lose its hydroplane lifting tendency should the craft start to fly, thus preventing the kind of accident which killed Donald Campbell in 1967.

Why the wheel-driven record?

Breedlove has always admired Campbell. When Craig stopped off in England during a world tour following his 407 record assault in 1963, Campbell—one of his chief rivals—threw a party in the young Californian's honor.

"I couldn't believe he would have a party for me after I'd broken the record," Breedlove recalls. "What was more amazing, he invited the press, even after the way they'd all been down on him and comparing him to me.

"And you know? In five minutes Campbell had the press falling all over him. He turned on the charm and started telling some of those great

Craig Breedlove and the "Spirit of America." *Courtesy Goodyear Tire and Rubber Company.*

Craig Breedlove checks wheels on "Spirit of America." *Courtesy Goodyear Tire and Rubber Company.*

Courtesy Goodyear Tire and Rubber Company.

Shaken by the death, Breedlove sent a cable of condolence to Campbell's widow, Tonia.

In the spring of 1969, Craig was a guest on a Los Angeles morning TV show, along with Tonia Bern Campbell, who had resumed her singing career. After the show, Breedlove asked her a question: ''Whatever happened to 'Bluebird'?''

Campbell's widow told him that the car was on display in a small museum at Surrey. At her suggestion, he flew to England and negotiated with

Craig Breedlove entering cockpit of ''Spirit of America.'' Courtesy Goodyear Tire and Rubber Company.

stories of his. And, hey, he was just as gracious as he could be toward me. I was afraid he'd look down his nose, or resent me, but he was just as gracious as could be.''

Less than four years later, Campbell was killed trying to exceed his own world water speed mark.

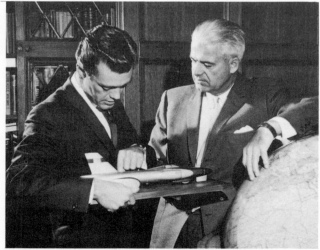

Craig Breedlove holds scale model of ''Spirit of America.'' Courtesy Goodyear Tire and Rubber Company.

the trustees of the estate to drive ''Bluebird,'' as soon as he could come up with a sponsor.

He figures it would take about $100,000 to take the jet car out of mothballs. With modifications, Breedlove believes ''Bluebird'' is capable of 475 miles an hour. One change would be to move the driver further to the rear.

''I couldn't believe how far forward Campbell had been sitting. Up there you don't feel what's going on because the skating and fishtailing all

Following a black line marked across the salt, Craig Breedlove roars into the start of the measured mile, marked by tiny
timing equipment and flags, at a speed above 400 mph.
Courtesy Goodyear Tire and Rubber Company.

takes place in the rear. What surprises me is that
Donald could have driven at that speed (403.1 in
1964).

Craig Breedlove's fascination with speed dates
back to his childhood. He was born March 23,
1937 in Costa Mesa, California.

"At first, I was more fascinated by the mechanical end of cars. The way I got started on them was
that the older kids in the neighborhood had a car
club called the "Igniters." I used to hang around
with them. I was about 12 and most of them were
16 or 17.

Craig Breedlove, after setting record of 468.72. *Courtesy Goodyear Tire and Rubber Company.*

"They took a liking to me. They'd take me to drag races on weekends. I got real interested. I talked my Mom into letting me get a car for my 13th birthday. I had a little money myself. At Christmas time, I asked for money instead of presents so I could save up for a car.

"I got a 1934 Ford for $75. I had about $45 and my Mom and stepdad gave me the other $30 for my birthday. Of course, I was too young to drive. I couldn't drive for three years. I had to promise I'd just work on the car.

"Well, I took that car completely apart—every piece. It was all over the place. I bought hot rod magazines and read all about hopping up cars. I bought special gears for the rear end and installed them. I cleaned the frame and repainted it. I got a supercharged '48 flathead Merc' engine.

"About all I wanted to do was to work on that car, but I didn't have any idea at all of driving."

When he was 16, Breedlove brought his hot rod to a race course at El Mirage Dry Lake—but not to drive it.

The "Spirit of America" completing a run at Bonneville. *Courtesy Goodyear Tire and Rubber Company.*

Not long before that he had driven a car in a race at Bonneville and finished eighth. "It scared me a little. The car slipped around a lot. I though it was kinda dangerous."

The "Spirit of America" and crew, preparing for the run which set a record of 526.26 mph. *Courtesy Goodyear Tire and Rubber Company.*

Craig Breedlove, prior to his 526.26 mph run. *Courtesy Goodyear Tire and Rubber Company.*

"El Mirage sort of scared me too. Everybody said it was a tricky course, so I lined up a guy to drive the car for me. But he was already driving some other cars and the association told him he couldn't take another one. So I gave it a try myself."

The reluctant young driver calmly went out and set a class speed mark of 142 miles an hour.

Breedlove graduated from Venice High school in California, majoring in drafting and machine shop, "so I could build parts for my racing cars."

Just out of high school, he spent his time around drag strips, working long hours on cars and performing a variety of mechanical jobs.

Subsequently he worked for two years at a Santa Monica firm that specialized in building race cars. Breedlove added to his store of skills by becoming an expert welder and learned many of the basic principles of speed-car building and design.

Later, he installed air conditioners, then worked in a parts department of an auto agency. From there he went to Douglas Aircraft as a structural technician.

In 1960 he joined the Costa Mese fire department. Why a fireman?

"To make more money. It was a good job. Nice pay, nice guys. But it was really boring. You sit there so long, and you're a kind of glorified janitor.

"I didn't think I was accomplishing anything where I was. I wanted to do something more important. I began thinking that a lot of young Americans were just as good at designing and building cars and souping up engines as were the racing teams of Europe.

"I became convinced that we could build a car that would capture the unlimited record for the measured mile. After all, we lacked only money.

"These ideas gradually jelled into the "Spirit of America" project. Deciding on the car's name was easy; the name tells the whole story.

"But it wasn't easy for a 22-year-old guy with no college education to go to a company and get them to believe in your idea."

Married at 17, he was divorced at 22, the father of three children. "My wife didn't understand what was inside me to do these things. Everybody wants to do something. People who haven't any drive never get anything done."

However, Craig's second wife, Lee (they were divorced in 1968) understood what he wanted. She had two children by a previous marriage and shared a love of speed. She was just the kind of encouragement Breedlove needed to launch his project.

His first thoughts were about a piston-powered, conventional streamliner. But he soon found out he could buy lots more horsepower for the same price in a jet engine. Further, a jet car would be simpler and far more efficient.

Breedlove drew up plans for such a car. But realizing his limitations as a designer, he turned to experts for help. Through his enthusiasm, he enlisted the aid of an aerodynamicist, a propulsion engineer, and a model builder. More than 100 wind

"Spirit of America" roars through the measured mile at 526.26 mph. *Courtesy Goodyear Tire and Rubber Company.*

"Spirit of America" crashes after run to cement 526.26 mph land-speed record. *Courtesy Goodyear Tire and Rubber Company.*

tunnel tests were run for design improvement.

At this point, two years after the start of the project, Breedlove's meager resources ran out.

During this time, the Breedloves learned to live with two air duct molds 10 feet long and weighing 1,000 pounds lying on the living room floor. Breedlove jacked up the rear wall of his garage, moved it back 21 feet and extended the roof to cover it. The garage now measured 41 feet by 20 feet and made the attached five-room house look like an appendage.

Rod Shapel, an automobile designer and project engineer at Task Corporation, drew up the first blueprints.

Art Russell, a model builder for Revell, carved a model out of pine to be used in wind-tunnel tests. Walt Sheehan, a Lockheed engineer, concocted the air ducts that led from the nose to the rear section and fed air to the jet engine.

The original engine came from Ed Perkins, a Los Angeles machine-shop owner and a bishop in the Mormon church.

Breedlove tried to interest major companies in the "Spirit," but met with no success until October of 1961.

Casting about for sponsors, he walked into the Santa Monica marketing district office of Shell Oil Company and asked to see the manager. Under one arm he carried a brochure, under the other was a box containing a model of his unique racer.

Craig Breedlove is congratulated by members of his crew after his 526.26 mph run and subsequent crash. *Courtesy Goodyear Tire and Rubber Company.*

Breedlove had incorporated theories in the building of the car that had yet to be proven on the salt. The car weighed nearly three tons, stood six-foot high, 35-feet long and 11 feet wide. It was quite an awesome-looking piece of machinery.

It was supported by only three wheels, one forward and two on a semi-rigid outrigger setup aft. None of these wheels were steerable.

He planned to steer by braking the two rear wheels independently, from floor-mounted panels, up to about 150. From then on, a Canard fin under the nose was expected to have enough bite in the slipstream to provide control via a conventionally mounted steering wheel. All braking was by parachute.

The "Spirit" was powered by a General Electric J-47 jet engine similar to the type used in an F-86D fighter plane.

On the dried-up bed of Lake Bonneville, the "Spirit" was given its first speed tests. While Breedlove drove it at an estimated 300 miles an

Thinking he was a Shell.dealer with the same name, the manager agreed to see Breedlove. But when he learned his error, the manager asked Craig to limit his call to 10 minutes.

Two hours later, Breedlove was still talking, and the manager, fascinated by the prospects and the young man's enthusiasm, was hooked.

Within three months, Shell had agreed to become a sponsor. Goodyear Tire and Rubber agreed to design and build the 48-inch tires, as well as machine the wheels and make the brakes.

Breedlove's partly-completed machine was moved from the garage behind his home to the shop of a leading builder of custom cars. For months the work went on.

In August of 1962, the $250,000 "Spirit of America" was loaded on a trailer and brought to the Salt Flats. Accompanying it was an expert crew of more than 20 men, equipped with everything from a complete machine shop to spare parts.

"It was handmade—I mean made with hand tools, a little file and a screwdriver," recalls Breedlove.

"The car was the equivalent of a prototype fighter plane that would take an aircraft company a million dollars, 20,000 men and all their machinery to build."

Craig Breedlove repairing "Spirit of America" following crash at Bonneville. *Courtesy Goodyear Tire and Rubber Company*

hour, numerous "bugs" hampered the car's performance.

Light crosswinds caused it to veer from the marked course. The different braking on the rear wheels, used instead of the steerable front wheel to maintain the car on course, was unable to correct the veering.

The only recourse was to return to the drawing board. New engineering talents were called in. The car was modified in various ways.

The front wheel was made steerable through two degrees in each direction. A six-foot-high vertical tail fin was added to increase stability and move the center of pressure to the rear. The industrial-type disc brakes were rigged to work from a single brake pedal. The throttle linkage was arranged for either hand or foot operation, where formally it was operated only by hand.

Late in July of 1963, the "Spirit" and her crew were back on the Flats. Breedlove reached a speed of 276 and reported no problems.

Five days later—August 5—the 25-year-old Californian climbed into the cockpit, pushed the throttle to a setting that represented 90 percent of the power, and moved down the track.

At that moment, he had driven the "Spirit of America" less than 200 miles in a total of 22 test runs.

Craig Breedlove tests the soft salt on which the "Spirit of America" came to a stop following the 1965 version of his "wild ride." His car, which became partially airborne at speeds estimated in excess of 600 mph, came to a halt 1-½ miles past the end of the track at the Bonneville Salt Flats. *Courtesy Goodyear Tire and Rubber Company.*

High speed stress shows both in the "Spirit of America" and the face of Craig Breedlove. *Courtesy Goodyear Tire and Rubber Company.*

Speed for the first run: 388.47. Quickly the car was turned around, refueled and ready for the all-important return trip.

This time Breedlove set the throttle at 95 percent power and roared through the measured mile at 428.37. The average for the two runs, calculated from the elapsed time of the two, was 407.45.

Craig Breedlove had broken the world land speed record set by the late John Cobb of England 16 years before. He was the fastest man on wheels.

But Breedlove wanted to go faster. "I don't think the limit has been reached yet. I think I can go faster. The course was bumpy, but the car held up well under the punishment."

He decided to return to the salt the next day. Then it was announced he would fly instead to New York for personal appearances. Shell and Goodyear wanted to take full advantage of the publicity.

Meanwhile, in Paris, the FIA said the "Spirit of America" was not an automobile and referred all questions concerning recognition of the record to the Federation Internationale Motorcyliste (FIM) in Geneva, Switzerland, which welcomed the sudden attention.

The FIM promptly created a turbine class to accomodate the three-wheeler.

In New York, Breedlove said: "I call it a car, because I built it as a car. As far as automobiles go, John Cobb's record still stands."

Late in 1963, after the furor over his achievement had subsided, the team of experts went back to work on Breedlove's car. The "Spirit" was given a new J-47 jet engine with 5,700 pounds of thrust instead of the 5,200 pounds of the previous engine. The nose was given a more streamlined configuration.

A new set of wheels and tires were installed, but not because of wear. They were taken out of service for historical and exhibition purposes.

In the meantime, others had set their sights on Breedlove's record. Walt Arfons prepared to run his Goodyear-sponsored "Wingfoot Express." His brother Art was ready in his Firestone-backed "Green Monster."

Heavy rains on the Salt Flats delayed the 1964 speed attempts for months. Not until late September was the track in shape for trials.

First the "Wingfoot," driven by Tom Green, set a new record of 413.20 on October 2. Three days later, Art Arfons fired his "Green Monster" to a two-way mark of 434.02.

His 1963 record exceeded twice within three

Craig Breedlove. *Courtesy Shell Oil Company.*

"Spirit of America-Sonic I."*Courtesy Goodyear Tire and Rubber Company.*

Craig Breedlove checks tires of "Spirit of America-Sonic I." *Courtesy Goodyear Tire and Rubber Company.*

days, Breedlove arrived at Bonneville with his crew on October 11.

Around-the-clock testing and tuning made the "Spirit" ready for its initial trials on October 13. Repeating his procedure of 14 months previous, Breedlove climbed into the cockpit, fastened his helmet and safety belts, and watched quietly as the cockpit canopy was installed.

This year he had an additional factor in his favor. The hydralic pressure on the brakes had been increased so he could hold the car motionless as he revved the jet engine to racing tempo.

With the brakes released, the "Spirit" sped down the 10-mile course toward the measured mile—4½ miles away. It shot through the traps at ever-increasing speed. Once past the second

Tires for "Spirit of America-Sonic I" were tested 850 mph. *Courtesy Goodyear Tire and Rubber Company.*

marker in the measured mile, Breedlove released the drag chute, which pulled down his speed to the point where he could apply the foot brake. His speed: 442.59.

While the special turbine fuel was poured in the gas tank for the return run, Breedlove made minor adjustments to the throttle setting. This time he clocked a faster 498.13 through the traps. His two-way average was 468.72.

Again Craig Breedlove was the fastest man on wheels. But neither he nor his crew were satisfied.

"I knew I had the record by the way the car performed. It ran beautifully and I managed to miss the rough spot on the course. I'm confident I can hit 500 miles an hour on land and I plan to stay until the job is done."

For 48 hours, almost without pause, the experts labored over the "Spirit." It was tuned to micrometric fitness.

On October 15, Breedlove streaked through the mile in 513.33—faster than any man had ever driven a car. Again came the fast turnabout, the

refueling, the resetting of the throttle to an even higher speed level.

As he rocketed past the marker at the end of the measured mile, the watchers anticipated the drag chute to billow out behind the flashing car. But it didn't.

Four-and-one-half miles further down the track, where Breedlove should have been coasting to a stop, he was still going at an estimated 300 miles an hour.

The "Spirit" yawed crazily downcourse. It hit and splintered a wooden utility pole, shot up an incline, soared over a six-foot dike and finally nosed down, three miles off course, in a canal of salt water 18 feet deep.

Breedlove managed to remove the canopy of the battered racer and swim to the side of the pool. He climbed onto the dike embankment as the first wave of men reached the scene.

Craig Breedlove checks out the jet-powered "Spirit of America," with his wife, Lee, in the cockpit. She drove the car to the women's world land speed record with a two-way average of 308.56 mph through the measured mile at Bonneville. She is the first woman ever to drive a car faster than 300 mph. *Courtesy Goodyear Tire and Rubber Company.*

They quoted Breedlove as saying: "Just let me kiss the ground. I almost drowned in that thing."

Witnesses said Breedlove appeared to be in a slight case of hysteria. They said he seemed happy to be out of the racer. And who could blame him?

Then he added, "For my next trick I'll set myself afire." When Bill Neely of Goodyear reached the scene, Breedlove told him: "I'm okay baby. What's my speed?"

He was timed at 539.89 through the mile for a two-way average of 526.26. Breedlove had to be coaxed into the ambulance. At nearby Wendover, it took him 30 minutes to convince the doctors he was okay. By nightfall the once-proud "Spirit of America" was finally pulled out of the lake.

It marked the last ride for the sleek three-wheeler that had thrilled the racing world and turned a hotrodder from California into an international hero.

While Breedlove publically announced it would take at least two years before he could return to the Flats, he already had plans for a faster, more powerful "Spirit."

By the time he returned to Utah in 1965, arch-rival Art Arfons had cracked Craig's land speed record by 10 miles with a 536.75 clocking.

Breedlove's "Spirit of America-Sonic I" was a 34-foot 7 inch four-wheeler with a needle nose and

Craig Breedlove (left) and Dean Moon (center) explain the aerodynamic design of Breedlove's "Spirit of America" rocket car, which he hopes to have built for record attempts in 1974.

a 10½-foot high tail. Power was supplied by a J-79 General Electric turbojet developing 15,000 pounds of thrust with a three-stage afterburner.

Breedlove felt confident the car had the capability to reach supersonic speed. But he was wrong. After setting land speed records of 555 and 600.601, sandwiched around Arfons' 576 effort, Breedlove admitted:

"The car we now have won't make it. We thought it would when we designed it, but from our experience, we know it won't. Parts of it have supersonic capability, but I don't want to say what it lacks. That's my secret."

But back to the fall of 1965. It was a tough October.

First, he couldn't understand why the engine held virtually the same speed, ranging between 514 and 518, while the power setting had been increased. The problem was diagnosed as engine backfire. That is, it de-accelerated while under full power. And even when the power mystery was solved and the adjustment made, the "Spirit" suffered heavy body stress during a 534 run when wind damage buckled the panels.

Then on October 21, the "Spirit" became partially airborne and careened out of control at 600 miles an hour. Breedlove, however, escaped injury when the car veered off course, whizzed between two telephone poles and stopped in the soft, mushy salt about 1½ miles beyond the end of the hard surface track.

During the scramble, Breedlove's parachute drag-braking system failed and he had to rely on the regular brakes to slow the car down.

"Thank God for good brakes. A lot of things went through my mind, including last year. Just say I'm lucky."

On November 3, Breedlove was ready for another record attempt. He hoped that special airfoils added to the front end would keep the wheels on the ground.

The device worked perfectly as Breedlove gunned his four-wheeler to a new record of 555.127 on bursts of 544.382 and 566.394.

The Californian was jubilant.

"I never had to work so hard for a record in my life. The car accelerated well and it was pretty smooth at 500 miles an hour. The track is drying out and was kind of like a washboard at the start.

"It's taken all year to build a new car and get the record back, so we intend to stay around. We'll run later this week for the 600 mark and make it tougher for Art."

But he didn't make any more runs. Instead, Breedlove waited to see if Arfons' "Green Monster" had enough power to continue the jet duel.

Craig had to wait just four days for the answer, as Arfons pushed his "Monster" to a new record of 576.533. But in the process, the car suffered a high-speed blowout and was extensively damaged. Arfons returned to Ohio to make repairs and wait for Breedlove's next move.

On Monday, November 15, Craig Breedlove took advantage of a break in the weather to regain his land speed title in a record-shattering 600.601 performance.

The runs of 593.178 and 608.201 were so smooth and effortless that Breedlove slowed down at the south end of the course, made a big sweeping turn, and parked the "Spirit of America-Sonic I" next to a moving-van that served as his mobile repair shop.

"Boy it's a great feeling. I'm sure we've got it for this year. Now let's see if ex-king Arthur comes back. That 600 is about a thousand times better than 599," he said with a wide grin across his beaming face.

Breedlove was asked how much faster the car could go on the Flats before it became too dangerous. He paused for a moment, then told reporters: "I don't know how much faster we can go, but we already have a definite problem with the Bonneville course. It's only 11 miles long and our greatest problem is getting stopped. There are longer tracks in Australia and Chile where we wouldn't have this braking problem.

"And don't talk about the sound barrier—740 to 760 on the Flats. That's a long way off."

Now the "long time off" seems to be right over the horizon.

And if Craig Breedlove has his way, the latest "Spirit of America" will join its illustrious ancestors in cracking another barrier that man once felt was far beyond his reach.

10
Art Arfons—The Ohio Hot-Rodder

One Sunday afternoon in 1954, Art Arfons and his wife, June, were out for a leisurely ride. Suddenly they were snarled in a traffic jam.

Curious to see what had caused the delay, Arfons decided to follow the long line. It took him to a drag race.

The sight of cars rumbling down the airport runway had a strange effect on the 28-year-old World War II veteran.

Within a week Art and his brother, Walt, had fashioned their first dragster out of junk parts. Soon Art was hitting 80 miles an hour.

The chance happening was to change his entire life. It took Art Arfons out of the family feed mill in Akron, Ohio, to instant stardom as a drag racer and ultimately as the fastest man on wheels.

Between October 1964 and November 1965, Arfons drove his jet-powered "Green Monster" to world land speed records of 434,536 and 576 miles an hour.

Arfons' "Monster," the car he affectionately called "my baby" met a violent death on November 17, 1966. Despite the 600 miles an hour crash, followed five years later by a drag strip accident which claimed the lives of three persons, Art Arfons doubts if he'll ever give up racing.

"Well, if you're gonna die anyway you might as well die doing what you want."

Despite his close calls with death, he shows no regrets.

"No, I wouldn't change a thing. I've been completely satisfied with my life. When you can make a living at your hobby for as many years as I have, it's gotta be good."

As a driver, Arfons realizes the risks involved in his sport. The deaths of others torment him.

In 1969, a young driver named Garth Hardacre was killed driving one of Arfons' dragsters. "Garth was almost like a son to Art," says his wife.

His appearance in Dallas, Texas in October of 1971 was to be his last. He had hoped to run the quarter-mile distance at 300 miles an hour in his latest jet, "Super Cyclops."

Instead, a tire blew during a run. The car veered sharply out of control, smashed through a guard rail and three persons were killed. The car was mangled beyond repair.

Physically, Arfons was just shaken up. Mentally, he lived in anguish for months. "The accident in Dallas about drove him crazy," points out June Arfons. "He just about went out of his mind."

"'Super Cyclops' hit 292 in Florida, 293 in North Carolina and 294 in Texas," brags Arfons. "The car had potential to run 320. I was never over 96 per cent power. You pressed the button and you had the whole works (all four stages of afterburner). That was the best handling car I ever built. I was gonna run 300, then hang it up. It was part of the deal."

After almost two decades of driving professionally, Art Arfons accepted his first full-time, non-racing job. Arfons is a salesman at an Akron speed shop called Art Arfons Associates. An out-of-town group put up the money to back the project only if he would quit racing for five years.

"I had to sign an agreement that I wouldn't drive a car if they put all this money in and put my name on it. I could go out, drive and break the contract—but this really the first time in my life that I've had hospitalization insurance and all that

Crew members service the Ford Daytona Coupe that set 23 endurance records at the Bonneville Salt Flats. Bobby Tatroe dives from behind the wheel and co-driver Craig Breedlove prepares to take over during a brief pit stop. The car averaged 150.094 miles for 12 grueling hours. *Courtesy Goodyear Tire and Rubber Company.*

stuff that goes with a job. It's a nice job.

"I was sick of the traveling, anyway. I was covering 60,000 miles a year and sometimes wouldn't be home for five weeks at a time. I wasn't enjoying the traveling, but I still enjoyed the driving."

Despite the job security, despite the regular hours, Art Arfons isn't satisfied. He looks at a massive intercontinenal missile laying on his workshop floor.

"It's out of a "Hound Dog" missile that's carried in the wing of a B-52. Drop it and it goes Mach 2.5—about 1,700 miles an hour.

"It'll be a dragster. Who knows? Once I get it

built, I might just sneak a ride in it and see how it feels."

Born February 3, 1926, in Akron, Art seemed to have a natural mechanical ability.

He took his first car apart when he was 11 years old. While a student at Springfield High School, Arfons signed up for special classes in welding and aircraft mechanics.

In 1943—when he was 17, Art talked his parents into letting him join the Navy at the end of his junior year. The Navy gave him more training in diesel mechanics.

Arfons went on to pilot a landing barge during the bloody assault on Okinawa. But his barge was

The Arfons brothers congratulate each other after brother
Arthur drove the "Green Monster" 144.95 mph at the finish
of a quarter-mile from a standing start. Left to right, Walt
Arfons, Arthur Arfons, and Dale Arfons. *Courtesy Art Arfons*.

different. He rigged a motor so none of his winchmen would be exposed to rifle fire.

Out of service, he returned to the family feed mill. On June 14, 1947, married June LaFontaine. (The marriage would produce three children).

Seven years later, his life changed with that one

Art Arfons. *Courtesy Firestone Tire & Rubber Company.*

visit to a local dragstrip. When Art returned home he told his brother, Walt, about the races. Walt, older by 10 years, became just as enthused. The next day they rummaged through the junk parts Art had collected over the years.

First, they got a 1940 Oldsmobile, then built a set of rails and installed the engine. Coupled to this was the rear end of a Packard they had picked up at a junk yard. They also had an extra airplane wheel on hand, so the Arfons Brothers welded it to the frame, and their car was now a three-wheeler.

Finally, they topped it all with some green tractor paint. It was the only paint they had available at the time.

A week later Art Arfons had seen his first drag race, he had a car on the track. He was 28 years old.

In its first appearance, the car drew laughs from the crowd. "It's a green monster," someone yelled.

"That's a mighty fine description," agreed the announcer. "Okay, folks here it comes—the 'Green Monster'."

In its maiden run, the "Monster shut down halfway down the strip. On its second try, Art hit 85, but the winner's time was 105. Thus, his first day as a drag racer had ended in failure.

The next year, the Arfons brothers were totally consumed in drag racing. By the middle of the summer, "Green Monster No. 2" was hitting peak speeds of more than 100 miles an hour.

After some local success, the Arfons brothers were brash enough to think they might have some luck at the World Series of Drag Racing in Lawrenceville, Illinois.

When the Series was over, Art's speed of 132.25 was the fastest. In 1956, Art and Walt Arfons decided to go their separate ways. With Walt out of the picture, the car-building was left to Art and his boyhood friend, Ed Snyder. Together, they turned out "Green Monster No. 6" which carried Art to his third straight World Series win. But even more important, Art Arfons became the first drag racer to break 150 in the quarter-mile. The car is on permanent display at the Museum of Speed in Daytona Beach, Florida.

Arfons continued to travel faster and faster, reaching 180 in "Green Monster No. 11," which was powered by a V-12 Rolls Royce engine, originally designed for a Mustang fighter plane.

In 1959, Art made a permanent contribution to drag racing by devising the braking parachute.

"I was making $55 at the mill, working 70 hours a week, six days a week. I started taking time off from the mill a week at a time in 1959. That's when 'No. 11' was running real good. That car put me in business. That's when I started getting calls and making money."

That's also about the time Arfons seriously began thinking of the world land speed record. His boyhood hero was John Cobb.

"I read everything they printed about him. When he and Eyston battled back and forth in 1939 I thought that was really something just for the man to climb down into a car wearing an old cloth helmet and goggles in a car that had no roll bar, no protection."

By the summer of 1960, Arfons had completed building his first Bonneville car, and it was easy to

Art Arfons in cockpit of first jet car, "Cyclops." *Courtesy Firestone Tire & Rubber Company.*

tell the Cobb influence. Arfons' "Anteater" resembled the famed "Railton Special" from the back.

Powered by a 24-cylinder Allison aircraft engine designed to power the B-29 bomber, the "Anteater" hit 260 before gear trouble forced Arfons back to Ohio.

Art's speed improved to 313.78 in 1961, But once again mechanical trouble ruined his bid. This time he burnt out a clutch.

To this day, Arfons insists the car can go faster.

"I still feel I can get 450 out of "Anteater." I never gave that car half a chance after 1961 and that's something I've regretted since. It was a good car.

"It wouldn't cost nothing to put it together. She ran real good at 300. She hit 313 in low gear and I never did get it into second. I'd just use one gear instead of two and gear it for 450."

To break the wheel-driven record, Arfons estimates he would need five miles of acceleration and 10 miles of salt.

In the winter of 1961, he bought an 8,000-horsepower J-47 jet engine, and "Cyclops" was born.

"I quit gambling with 'Cyclops.' I knew what I was getting before I made a run. I've run that car four years with the same engine. Never had any trouble with it." By 1962, Art Arfons was one of the biggest names in drag racing and commanded a fee of $750-$1,000 for three exhibition runs down the strip.

"Cyclops" at Bonneville. *Courtesy Firestone Tire & Rubber Company.*

Art Arfons in "Anteater," his first land speed car. *Courtesy Firestone Tire & Rubber Company.*

to pieces, some of the parts flying into a field 30 feet away.

In August of 1962 Arfons returned to Bonneville but fell short of the land-speed record. Yet his 343.88 clocking was a milestone. It was the fastest anyone had traveled in an open-cockpit car.

Now a money-making professional drag racer, Arfons was appearing in Denver, Colorado when his big break came in November. A dealer in Florida contacted Art and told him a J-79 engine was available. Built by General Electric at an original cost of $250,000, the 17,500-horsepower jet powerplant had been used in B-58 bombers and

"Cyclops" was quite a crowd-pleaser with its one eye piercing the darkness as it reached speeds of 240 miles an hour. But it was more than just a dragster. "Cyclops" was also a genuine land speed contender.

Arfons added an afterburner when the car hit only 196 on its first test run. He tested the burner behind his shop at Pickle Road. It was quite a test as the engine's blast blew out windows and picked up the chicken house, some 100 feet away, and moved it five feet over some trees. The house fell

Art Arfons is shown with "Anteater." *Courtesy Firestone Tire and Rubber Company.*

Left, Art Arfons, "Anteater." Right, "Doc" Nathan Ostich, "Flying Caduceus." *Courtesy Firestone Tire & Rubber Company.*

F-104 fighter planes and was capable of air speed exceeding 1,400 miles an hour.

Arfons now had the engine he needed for the land speed record and purchased the damaged J-79 for $5000. Sixty-seven blades had to be straightened out. It took 10 painstaking days to complete the job.

Purchasing another J-79 in Indiana, Arfons and Ed Snyder tore down the two engines. In two weeks the jigsaw puzzle had been completed. Art now had the most powerful engine ever to hit the Bonneville Salt Flats.

Some 12 months and 5,000 man-hours later, "Green Monster" (No. 15) had been built without even a blueprint.

Arfons' simulated test run once again took place

behind his shop. The car was chained to two giant oak trees. Arfons started the ''Monster'' and a flame shot out, burning up trees and undergrowth for 150 feet. Even without unleashing the four-stage afterburner, the noise was so deafening and vibrating that a woman a mile away thought her furnace had blown up and called a repairman. There were reports that people as far away as three miles had also heard the blast.

Thus was born the world's smallest, cheapest and three times fastest land speed car.

He built the ''Green Monster'' 21 feet long be-

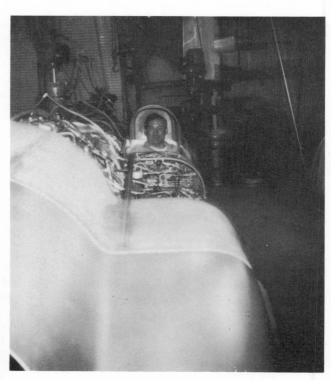

Arfons sits in cockpit of ''Green Monster.''

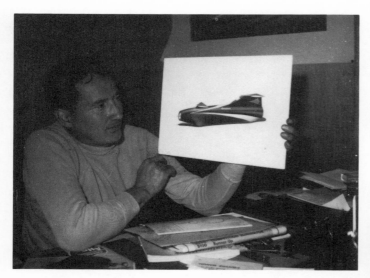

Art Arfons holds sketch of jet-powered ''Green Monster No. 2.''

cause it wouldn't have otherwise fit into the bus he used to transport the car to Utah.

The government spent $1,000 to build an ejection system. Arfons paid $3 for a sawed-off shotgun which he fired to eject two chutes. An intricate metal-forming machine sold for $10,000. Art built one for $36. An axle came from a 1951 Dodge truck, a steering system from a '55 Packard, the instrument panel from an old airplane. He even repaired his tattered and torn used chutes on an old-fashioned sewing machine.

Aerodynamic engineers maintained that in order to go 500 miles an hour, Arfons would have to build a car one inch off the ground for every foot of length.

Twenty-one inches off the ground? Don't be

''Green Monster.''

absurd. Three-quarters of an inch was more like it.

On October 2, 1964, Walt Arfons' jet-powered "Wingfoot Express," driven by Tom Green, set a new land speed mark of 413.02 on runs of 406.5 and 420.7.

Three days later, Art hit 394.34 on his first burst across the Flats. Twenty-five minutes later, he gunned the "Green Monster" to 479. His two-way average was 434.02.

Arfons had made just four practice runs before setting his first of three land-speed records.

Firestone racing engineers who assisted the Ohio hotrodder estimated he used about 10,000 horsepower on his 479 solo.

With the Flats his private speedway for five more days, Art Arfons was determined to push the record far out of Craig Breedlove's reach.

Two days after he set the record—October 7—Arfons decided to go for the 500 barrier.

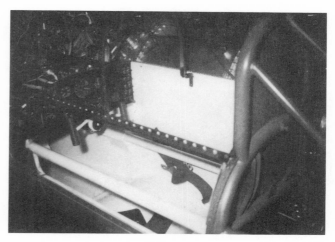

Cockpit of "Green Monster."

Unknown to Art, his long-time friend Chuck Mayenschein of Dayton, Ohio had hopped into the unoccupied right cockpit and had the ride of his

"Green Monster," being built in Art Arfons' workshop.

"Green Monster" under construction.

"Green Monster No. 2." *Courtesy Firestone Tire & Rubber Company.*

"Green Monster" under construction.

Arfons and "Green Monster." *Courtesy Firestone Tire & Rubber Company.*

Art Arfons. *Courtesy Firestone Tire & Rubber Company.*

life. Mayenschein brought a small tape recorder into the cockpit to record his reactions as the "Green Monster" hit 413 miles an hour.

When the run was over, Art climbed out of his cockpit and went around the other side of the car to confer with the Firestone engineers and his crew. That's when he saw Mayenschein, still strapped in the cockpit and wearing a mile-wide grin. All Arfons could say was "you crazy son of a gun."

Mayenschein had more than a passing interest in "Green Monster." He not only made the wooden scale-model of the car but helped with the body work.

With the help of three crew members, he laid his plans to hitch-hike a ride. After that incident, Arfons made sure the right-side cockpit was empty before he made a run.

After his 413 stroll, Arfons made several more runs, including a 468 clocking. Then he gently brought the "Monster" to 400 — 430 — 470 — 490 — with still a half-mile separating him from the timing zone.

Just as the speed indicator nudged the 500 mark, Arfons felt an overpowering jerk on the right side of the car. The pull was so strong Art thought the axle had broken and that he had lost the entire rear wheel.

Finally stopping the crippled car, Arfons was relieved to find out that only the right rear tire had blown. Further inspection of the car brought deeper concern. Damage to the right side, caused when 200 pounds of pressure of the front tire dug up a stray bolt somewhere on the course and shot it back like a bullet toward the rear tire, meant a long trip back home and two weeks of repair work.

In the meantime, Breedlove and his three-wheeled "Spirit of America" bettered Arfons' record by 34 miles an hour with his 468.72 round trip.

Forty-eight hours later — October 13 — Breedlove increased the record to an astouding 526.26, but wrecked his jet on the final run through the clocks.

Arfons was back on the Flats by October 25. Two days later he regained the record with a 536.75 average. His first run was 515.98.

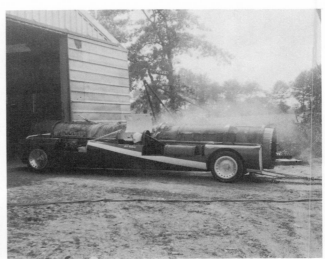

Art Arfons fires up "Green Monster" behind his garage. Car is chained down.

Art Arfons tests cockpit of "Green Monster."

"Green Monster" suffered another high-speed blowout and crashed into a course marker. Arfons was not hurt, but the right side of the car was badly damaged.

"A lot of things went through my mind when I climbed into the cockpit. I was the loneliest guy in the world. My crew and the Firestone engineers had asked me to make a few practice runs and then go for the record.

"I thought about and realized that it had been a year since I'd run at record speeds. My wife, June, was back in Akron expecting our third child and I didn't want to cause her any more worry. I just wanted to get it over with."

Because of the choppy condition of the salt,

A high-speed blowout on the return run silenced the screaming "Monster," but not before he had turned in a blistering 559.18. He would hold that record for more than a year.

On November 3, 1965, Breedlove regained his title as the fastest man on wheels when he averaged 555.127. His record lasted only 72 hours.

With two quick bursts of 575.724 and 577.386, the land-speed crown returned to Ohio. Average speed: 576.533. But in cementing the record, the

Test firing of "Green Monster" at Akron City Airport.

Art Arfons hooks up motor to nose of "Green Monster" to start the car.

Arfons used only two miles of running room before hitting the measured mile.

"The first run, despite the bumpy track, was great. I nosed the car up and held my speed between 560 and 590. I only went into minimum burner."

On the return trip, Arfons used only 1¾ miles for his approach. "When Ed (Snyder) told me I had to use a shorter approach because of the rough salt, this really shook me up. It meant going into afterburner full blast and accelerating as rapidly as possible. The acceleration was so great, I thought I was going through the back of the car. I kept

going faster, faster, faster, and realizing this was my chance and I'd better do it now."

How did he feel when it was all over?

"Great but tired and relieved. It isn't something I'd want to go through every day. I wasn't in the car but a minute or so—but it seemed like an eternity."

Art Arfons with "Green Monster." *Courtesy Firestone Tire & Rubber Company.*

"Green Monster" (left), with one of Art's dragsters. *Courtesy Firestone Tire & Rubber Company.*

Eight days later — November 15, 1965 — Breedlove drove his new "Spirit of America-Sonic I" to a new record of 600.601.

Could Art Arfons again regain his title?

On November 17, 1966, Arfons and his modified "Monster"—complete with dual tires and a second airfoil—crashed at speeds exceeding 600

Art Arfons and "Green Monster." *Courtesy Firestone Tire & Rubber Company.*

"Green Monster." *Courtesy Firestone Tire & Rubber Company.*

Art Arfons and his stable of hot cars. *Courtesy Firestone Tire & Rubber Company.*

"Green Monster" roaring down strip at Firestone's Fort Stockton, Texas testing track, enroute to drag strip record.

Instrument panel of "Green Monster."

"Green Monster" during run at Firestone Test Track.
Courtesy Firestone Tire & Rubber Company.

"Green Monster" at Bonneville. *Courtesy Firestone Tire & Rubber Company.*

miles an hour. Miraculously, Art escaped death.

It was a sudden gust of wind which forced him off course and triggered the wildest ride in land speed history.

"It was a freak accident and I think it would be a million-to-one chance you could ever do that again—I mean walking away from an accident at that speed. I think it won't ever happen again.

"Actually, I've had closer calls. Maybe it wasn't as spectacular, but I flipped end-over-end 14 times in a dragster back in 1957. I was only going about 160.

"I had skull and back injuries. I saw the trees growing out of the sky and I knew something was upside down. It was my first attempt to go light. I built that darned "Baloney Slicer" too light and it just came apart. There was nothing left to it."

That day, Arfons and Don "Big Daddy" Garlits were waging quite a duel, with Garlits going just a shade faster at 176. Determined to beat his arch rival, Art pushed the machine to full power.

Nine years later, Arfons was just as determined to beat his land speed nemesis, Craig Breedlove.

Everybody wanted Arfons to quit—his wife, his mother, his pals, his sponsor and even a former land speed adversary—but he wouldn't hear of it.

Perhaps Dr. Nathan Ostich, the man who introduced jets to land speed racing, put it best when he said:

"He has used up eight of his nine lives. He should save the last one for himself and his family. He doesn't need another fast ride. He should let the other guys have it."

No sooner, it seems, had Arfons returned home

to recuperate when he began making plans for a new "Green Monster." He even thought about attacking the world speed record on water.

Arfons' "boat" was nothing more than his jet car "Cyclops" mounted on a pair of 26-foot long aluminum pontoons, with two front-wheel tires.

Why tires?

"When I hit about 100 miles an hour," he explained, "the front end will lift out of the water and the tires will act as cushions. It's gonna ride like a baby buggy.

"I don't like boats really. But I want to prove my theory.

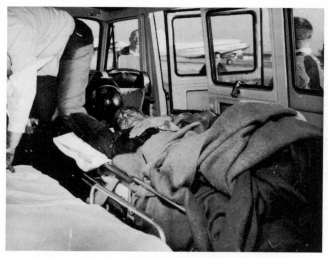

Art Arfons in ambulance at Salt Lake City, following crash of "Green Monster." *Courtesy Deseret News, Salt Lake City, Utah.*

However, that doesn't mean he's given up all hope of setting a new water-speed record.

On January 15, 1969, Arfons triggered his new "Green Monster" to a new world quarter-mile record from a standing start—267—at Firestone's seven-mile test track in Fort Stockton, Texas. It took just 6.4 seconds for the snarling 5,810-pound

"Green Monster" pops parachute during 1965 run. *Courtesy Firestone Tire & Rubber Company.*

In January of 1967, Arfons' hybrid creation passed its first test as it floated in perfect balance during a 30-minute test on a chemical pond behind Firestone's plant.

When the weather became warmer, he took his 8,000-horsepower "Green Submarine" for a 15-25 mile-an-hour test run on a small lake outside of Akron. It was like a kid playing with a new toy.

But when he couldn't find a sponsor, Art took off the pontoons and changed "Cyclops" back to a dragster.

"It's stupid to take a chance for nothing. If I tried to do it alone, it would cost about $10,000 to run the boat. There's the cost of getting to the water, plus keeping a crew. You could sit a month waiting for the right weather."

Rear end of wrecked "Green Monster." Note wheels and tires ripped from car. *Courtesy Firestone Tire & Rubber Company.*

113

Rear of wrecked "Green Monster." *Courtesy Firestone Tire & Rubber Company.*

Battered cockpit of "Green Monster." *Courtesy Firestone Tire & Rubber Company.*

Parts of "Green Monster" strewn about behind Art Arfons' garage.

Demolished "Green Monster," back in Art Arfons' garage.

Frontal view of Art Arfons' demolished "Green Monster,"
Nov. 17 1966. *Courtesy Deseret News, Salt Lake City, Utah.*

Artist's conception of car which Art Arfons believes will carry him past 1000 mph. *Courtesy Firestone Tire & Rubber Company.*

a lot cleaner, with less frontal area. I think it's better."

The familiar wing or airfoil is still there, designed to keep the car's front end from lifting.

The car is on display at Arfons' speed shop. Like its well-known master, it is temporarily grounded.

For how long? Only Art Arfons knows.

17,500-horsepower jet engine hangs in Art Arfons's garage workshop. It's a J-79 military engine with a four-stage afterburner.

jet to complete the distance. In November of that year, Arfons hit 273.55 at Rockingham, North Carolina.

"That little S-O-B don't know when to quit," he chuckled," just like it's daddy."

The Monster was almost 2,600 pounds lighter than its famed predecessor. "It's lighter, smaller,

11
WHOOSH—The Jet Era Is Born

The name of Dr. Nathan Ostich doesn't appear in the land speed record books. It's not because he didn't try. For three years, the Los Angeles physician waged a game battle in the world's first jet-powered land speed contender, the "Flying Caduceus."

Ostich caught the speed bug in 1949. No stranger to the Flats, he had raced there for 10 years and traveled 189.98 in a modified sedan—"as fast as the car could go."

But his "Flying Caduceus" was no modified sedan. It was a 28-foot long, needle-nosed car powered by a GE turbo jet engine, the type used in B-36 bombers. Two years in the building, the jet boasted a 5000 horsepower punch. Windtunnel tests at California Poly Tech showed the car had a speed potential of 500 miles per hour.

"Our goal is 500." said Ostich early in 1960. "We expect to begin testing within a couple of months." Then he explained that his $100,000 creation differed from Mickey Thompson's "Challenger I," which set an American record, in 1959, of 363.67, but fell short of its 400 goal.

"We will be straight jet-propelled, eliminating the problem of a transmission, which Mickey had. We also will have open wheels. The car looks like an airplane fuselage on wheels."

Ostich would be joined in the high-speed chase by Donald Campbell, Athol Graham, Art Arfons and Thompson.

In December of 1959, Graham had pushed his home-made "City of Salt Lake" to a top speed of 344.761. One year later, he felt certain his Allison-powered racer would capture the record.

On August 1, the 36-year-old Salt Lake City garageman, who had dreamed from boyhood of becoming the first American to drive 400 miles an hour, was killed. Graham was two-thirds of the way between the starting pit and the measured mile posts, traveling at an estimated 300, when his 4200-pound car skidded and flipped. When it came to a halt upside down, the car's body was broken and the wheels bent. A tow truck lifted the battered "City of Salt Lake" onto its right side, so Graham could be removed.

Graham, with a fractured skull, collapsed lung and other injuries, was flown to Salt Lake City, 125 miles away. He died at the hospital. His 29-year-old wife, Zeldine, was at the finish line waiting for her husband to complete his first run. "The car started to disintegrate," she said, "then it turned over. I couldn't see anything for the dust."

A crosswind with gusts estimated up to 25 miles an hour was buffeting the track during his attempt. The wind was believed a major cause of the crash.

Less than two months following her husband's death, Zeldine Graham said she would rebuild the car.

Ostich was next on the Flats. However, his 5000 horsepower jet was plagued by mechanical problems. Although the Los Angeles general practitioner pushed the car to 300 miles an hour, violent vibrations forced him back home.

While the car failed, the jet era had been officially launched.

Arfons, relying on an Allison aircraft engine for power, was forced to quit because of transmission trouble. His top speed in the "Anteater was 260.

Back at the Flats in 1960, Thompson had added

a supercharger to each of his four Pontiac engines. In addition, he covered the front wheels to improve streamlining.

Everything had gone wrong for three weeks. Then on September 9, Mickey pushed "Challenger" to a speed of 406.60—the fastest ever recorded. However, a broken transmission shaft

Dr. Nathan Ostich, 50-year-old Los Angeles physician, sits in the driver's seat of his partially-assembled "Flying Caduceus." *Courtesy Firestone Tire & Rubber Company.*

aborted his return run, thus preventing him from a new two-way record.

Now it was up to Campbell and his jet-powered "Bluebird."

The son of the legendary Sir Malcolm had already owned the speed record on water. He was determined to hold the land record as well—duplicating his father's feat.

Although the "Bluebird" was powered by a gas turbine engine, the car met FIA's international rules, since 40 percent of the 4,250 horsepower was transmitted directly through the wheels. In contrast, Ostich's jet was driven by pure thrust.

Campbell's plan was to gradually increase his speed. Within three days—September 12 to 15—he had pushed the speed indicator from 179 to 250. By his fifth run, Campbell had hit 300 and all appeared to be working well.

The next run was to be an acceleration test, followed by an official record attempt. Reaching a speed of 350-360 miles an hour, "Bluebird" suddenly spun, rolled on its right side and flipped in the air. Campbell escaped with a hairline skull fracture while the jet was badly damaged.

Despite the crash, he was convinced "Bluebird" had sufficient power to set the record. Four years later he would prove himself right.

When the 1960 speed season ended, John Cobb's 394 record had successfully withstood another challenge.

Poor salt conditions in 1961 virtually eliminated all record attempts. However, Art Arfons, driving his Allison-powered "Anteater," managed to hit 313.78 before a burned-out clutch knocked him out of action.

Pre-race publicity heralded 1962 as a banner year, with no less than 10 competitors—including seven jet cars. The cast included Thompson, Arfons, Ostich, Craig Breedlove, Glenn Leasher, Bob Knapp, Bill Frederick, Ernie Immerso and Bob Funk.

In addition, the car that carried Athol Graham to his death in 1960 had been rebuilt and was reported ready to return to Bonneville. It was quite an array of hardware.

Breedlove, a 24-year-old Californian, was building his three-wheeler, "Spirit of America." Arfons had abandoned conventional power and was readying his jet-thrust "Cyclops." Dr. Ostich was back with his "Flying Caduceus". Leasher was set to drive the jet-powered "Infinity." Thompson was ready with his "Challenger."

In addition, Knapp was constructing a four-ton monster, propelled by a pair of J-47 jet engines. Frederick was also relying on jet power, but his entire machine was to weigh 2960 pounds—including fuel. Immerso had a car driven by four Ford powerplants. It was a scaled-up version of his old twin-engine machine. Funk was also working on a four-engine creation.

But by countdown, five jets, plus Thompson's "Challenger" and Graham's "City of Salt Lake" were involved in the dangerous game.

By August 9, the "Flying Caduceus" had prog-

Dr. Nathan Ostich. *Courtesy Firestone Tire & Rubber Company.*

ressively increased its speed from 206 to 324 miles an hour. Now Ostich was ready to turn on full power.

Reaching a speed of 331 after about seven miles, the car suddenly went into a spectacular slide. The left front wheel snapped off. Finally, the 52-year-old driver fired his safety chute and the 6500-pound jet came to a halt. Ostich said he sensed trouble when the racer began veering to the right as he passed the three-mile marker on the 12-mile long straightaway.

"I had trouble pulling it back on course and then started shutting off power. It still wouldn't come back so I popped the chute.

"I felt the car spinning and I thought I was going into a roll. I did everything automatically—the

things I had learned in numerous practice runs. I didn't know I lost the wheel until I felt the car go down."

Ostich had only one thought during the slide.

"I didn't want to burn. That was the one thing on my mind and I remember grabbing for the extinguisher overhead."

Although he wasn't injured and the car suffered minor damage, the Los Angeles doctor and his crew headed back home to modify the jet. He was through for 1962.

"At high speed it is impossible to control the car with wheels," he explained. "At speeds between 319 and 324, it handled perfectly. But if you get the least little bit out of line, say only two degrees, there's 19,000 pounds of pressure pushing on one side. There's just no way to hold it. At high speed the only thing you can do is control it with a rudder.''

Why the spin? The left front wheel spindle had broken off, causing the wheel to come loose. As a result, the excessive transfer to the left front of the car when it began slipping sideways caused the break. It marked Ostich's 13th run on the Flats.

mented the youngster. "My parents say it's okay and I'm most eager to drive the car."

Anzjon successfully passed the 250 mile-an-hour hurdle when the car suffered a blowout. The only damage was to the skin, which was ripped by the pressure of the blowout.

In the winter of 1962, Otto Anzjon died of leukemia.

Dr. Nathan Ostich in the ''Flying Caduceus.'' *Courtesy Firestone Tire & Rubber Company.*

Despite 8,000 horsepower, the jet-thrust ''Cyclops'' didn't have enough fuel capacity and Arfons could only record a two-way average of 330.13.

Otto Anzjon, a 19-year-old mechanic from Salt Lake City, had rebuilt Athol Graham's ''City of Salt Lake.'' ''The idea of rebuilding the car was all Otto's,'' said Mrs. Graham. ''I would never have asked him to race but he has expressed a strong desire to fulfill Athol's lifetime dream.''

''I guess I should be scared but I'm not,'' com-

Breedlove, a newcomer to land speed racing, was at Bonneville with a three-wheeler which looked like an exotic plane without wings. Plagued by steering troubles, Breedlove reached only 300.

Now the spotlight was on Glenn Leasher and ''Infinity.''

The 26-year-old San Francisco driver and part-owner of ''Infinity'' was two-tenths of a mile through the measured mile when his jet car exploded at speeds exceeding 300 miles an hour. Ob-

Dr. Nathan Ostich and his crew. *Courtesy Firestone Tire & Rubber Company.*

servers said he entered the measured mile with afterburner on, but shut it off just after passing the marker. Whether of not he sensed trouble and was cutting the engine could not be determined. Leasher was killed instantly as "Infinity" was turned into a mass of twisted junk. The date: September 10, 1962.

"Everything appeared to be working all right when he suddenly disappeared in smoke and flame," said USAC's David Petrali, who was manning the telephone nearest the crash site. "Then the car started tumbling."

The day before the fatal crash, Leasher had made three runs, including a 330 sortee. He made a preliminary run of 283 to test the parachute brakes just prior to his death.

Leasher, who had been driving dragsters and jalopies since he was 15, was attempting something revolutionary in land-speed racing. He revved up the engine while keeping the wheels locked with his brakes and gave himself about a half-mile running distance before entering the measured mile. While this practice was common in drag racing, it was new on the Flats.

In August, 23-year-old Chuck Hatcher of North Hollywood, California, had recorded a 300 clocking on a test run.

Bill Frederick, the 21-year-old car owner from Woodland Hills, California, felt confident his "Valkyrie I" would crack the existing land speed record.

"She drove straight as an arrow and I know she'll go faster," he said.

As a result of Leasher's death, Frederick found himself without insurance. "The accident soured them (insurance companies) on another try now with a jet. Jet cars are a new thing and they aren't used to them yet. We'll just have to wait for next year."

Despite his optimism and the speed potential of his car, Bill Frederick did not return to the salt flats the next year. As a matter of fact, he never did challenge the world land speed record with jet-propulsion.

Now, a decade later, Frederick is readying a 1,000 mile an hour rocket racer, "Courage of Australia II," for the biggest challenge of all—breaking the sound barrier.

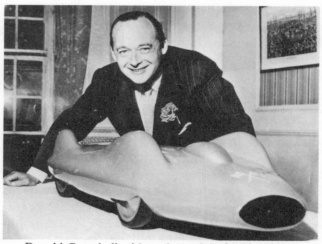

Donald Campbell with scale model of "Bluebird."

12
Yankee Doodle Dandy

A game 55-year-old doctor, a humiliated 26-year-old drag racer, a 46-year-old speed veteran, the widow of a land speed aspirant. They all came to Bonneville in 1963.

Dr. Nathan Ostich was at the Flats with his "Flying Caduceus." Young Craig Breedlove and his "Spirit of America," a wingless F-104 Starfire, were a big flop in 1962. Now he was back with a modified monster.

Walt Arfons, the Ohio grandfather who built the first jet dragster in 1959, was making his first Salt Flats appearance.

Zeldine Graham, widow of Athol Graham, had rebuilt her husband's piston-powered car. Driver Harry Muhlbach would to try to fulfill Graham's dream of a land speed record.

Driven by 30-year-old Tom Green, Arfons' "Wingfoot Express" had the first crack. However, the 8,000-horsepower jet was knocked out of contention after only four runs when salt was sucked into the engine.

Next it was Breedlove's turn. He was hoping for better things and not a repeat of 1962, when his mechanics couldn't even get the jet engine started. Steering problems had developed in the car's radical guidance system, which used wheel brakes and a canard fin with all three wheels fixed.

Newsmen gave up after the three-wheeler failed time after time to even make it through the timing clocks. One run was a 240 success. The rest of the time Breedlove veered from the course at speeds up to 300 miles an hour, by his own estimate.

"The Spirit of America" was unceremoniously removed from the Flats. "I was extremely disappointed," Breedlove said, reflecting on the events of 1962.

But this was another year—and a new "Spirit."

The front wheel was made steerable through two degrees in each direction; a six-foot high vertical tail fin was added to increase stability and move the center of pressure to the rear; the industrial-type disc brakes were rigged to work from a single brake pedal; the throttle linkage was arranged for either hand or foot operation, where formerly it was operated only by hand.

Late in July of 1963, "Spirit" and her crew were back on the Flats. Numerous test runs and minor adjustments were made. On July 31, Breedlove drove his 35-foot long jet to a speed of 276 and reported no problems. In all, he made 22 practice runs before he was ready to shoot for a record that had stood for 16 years.

On August 4, Breedlove unofficially hit 365.93 and set five records in the newly created USAC jet class. His marks were 335.6 in the kilometer, 356.4 in the mile, 330.52 for five kilometers, 313.1 for five miles and 287.36 for 10 kilometers.

Craig was confident of faster things to come.

"We have a steerable nose-wheel now and it has been great in practice runs. The six-foot high tail fin has been a big help in guiding the 'Spirit'."

It was August 5, 1963. At 3:30 a.m., the crew made the 11-mile drive from Wendover to the Salt Flats to make last-minute preparations. About two hours later, Breedlove arrived. He said, "I had a sip of water for breakfast and I feel fine."

Breedlove joked with his crew by putting on an old G.I. helmet shortly before he stepped into the cockpit at 6:30. He turned to a crowd of photographers and newsmen.

"I don't know why everyone is out here. We're just continuing our normal speed buildup."

Walt Arfons and his steam-powered dragster. Bob Tatroe driving. *Courtesy Goodyear Tire and Rubber Company.*

Rear end of Walt Arfons' steam dragster. *Courtesy Goodyear Tire and Rubber Company.*

Walt Arfons' steam-powered dragster. *Courtesy Goodyear Tire and Rubber Company.*

But everyone there, including USAC and FIM officials, knew otherwise. They knew this would be a run for the record.

In a raspy voice, USAC official L.T. Torros announced:

"Zero (wind) at the south test and she's all clear."

Slowly the "Spirit" began to move. Then it gathered momentum and in a matter of seconds was out of sight.

"The measured mile was 11 miles long but the first two miles were too rough to use. I was starting at the two mile mark, and even so, the salt was bumpy enough to bounce the "Spirit" several times while accelerating toward the other part of the track ahead of me.

"Salt began whirling around the cockpit, whipped up and powered by the front wheels. In spite of the cotton I had pushed into my ears inside the crash helmet I could hear the scream of the jet's compressor and some of its exhaust roar. The hard tires crunching on the salt, even the rattle and the bang of components inside the car were audible. And the ride, like all the others was rough as well as noisy.

"Breedlove's first run, using about 90 percent of the car's total power, lasted 9.267 seconds through the flying mile. The speed: 388.47.

"I started the run several feet to the right of the center stripe and the wind soon drifted me across the line. I stayed there. The car was still accelerating when I went through the light beam that marked the end of the measured mile and the kilometer. But by now, only four miles of salt were left and it was time to start shutting down.

"I took my foot off, coasted until I was approaching the 10-kilo marker and then pushed the steering wheel knob that flames out the engine and jettisons the drag-chute door.

"When the door popped open it deployed an eight-foot chute that served as a high-speed brake. The chute whipped around quite a bit and swerved the car from side to side, but I wasn't nervous. When the speed got down under 150, I began using the foot brakes and rolled to a stop alongside the vehicles at the far end of the course."

For the return run, Breedlove increased the power setting to 95 percent.

"By now the wind was freshening. Gusts were spilling out of a canyon west of the slat flats and creating crosswinds of seven and eight miles an hour on the course.

"I waited in the cockpit for awhile, then the reports showed that the wind had dropped to five miles an hour. It was time to go. From now on the winds would get stronger.

"I started the return run well over to the right of the center line and it's a good thing I did. By the time I entered the measured mile the wind had

Walt Arfons' steam-powered dragster. *Courtesy Goodyear Tire and Rubber Company.*

drifted the car 40 feet to the left, close to the markers and the rough salt outside the smoothed course. I corrected slowly and kept my foot on the floor, still accelerating.

"The 'Spirit' was traveling about 440 miles an hour at the end of the measured mile and I was just taking my foot off the throttle when the car began a slight weaving motion."

He knew what the trouble was at once—the chute door had popped open again and released the chute. Craig felt sure of a new record for the mile but thought he might miss new records for other distances. The chute was dragging the speed down rapidly.

There was a long wait at the south end after "Spirit" came to a halt. Joe Petrali and his USAC timing crew were inspecting the tape and averaging them and translating the time into speed.

Craig Breedlove had blasted through the measured mile in 8.404 seconds, or 428.37. His two-way record was 407.45.

Walt Arfons' jet dragster duel "Avenger" (with tail) vs.
"Green Monster." *Courtesy Walt Arfons Enterprises.*

Breedlove was jubilant as he emerged from the cockpit.

"It feels great," he said to the 200 spectators. "I had a lot of throttle left and the car came through in fine shape. I'm certain I can go much faster."

While Breedlove wanted to stick around to increase his speed record, Shell Oil—his chief sponsor—decided to leave well enough alone.

Technically speaking, John Cobb still held the wheel-driven mark of 394. But to the world, Craig Breedlove was the fastest on wheels.

Dr. Nathan Ostich tried to silence the critics by saying: "The main thing is you have to just get up there and drive."

Donald Campbell, another land-speed rival, praised the gutsy Californian. He called it a "jolly good effort."

Breedlove said, "I call it a car because I built it as a car—as far as automobiles go, John Cobb's record still stands."

In 1960, Zeldine Graham vowed to rebuild the ill-fated "City of Salt Lake." She believed the car had a 420 potential. Three years later, the flaming red racer was ready for the assault. On October 12, the hard-luck car went out of control and slid 1,000 feet on its top before coming to a halt. Harry Muhlbach escaped without injury.

There was no fire and most of the outside

aluminum covering "City of Salt Lake" was still intact, although bent considerably. The Allison aircraft engine appeared undamaged.

The car was on its first run of the day. Muhlbach had just passed the measured mile when the four-wheeler went into a half-mile long skid, rolled over twice and landed upside-down. The slightly stunned driver said the tachometer was on about 4,250 or 4,300 RPM and figured he was doing "above 395 miles an hour" when he crashed.

However, Joe Petrali, chief steward for USAC, said the timers calculated he was "doing 240 sideways" during the wild gyrations.

Reason for the crash: the braking parachute accidentally popped out, sending the car careening

The "Wingfoot Express." *Courtesy Goodyear Tire and Rubber Company.*

out of control. It was the same problem that had haunted him for four days.

"I just about lost it twice Friday (October 11) because the chute was out," Muhlbach said after the crash. He dragged the parachute for 10 miles down the track during a preliminary run and was unable to get above 200. As in the crash, he was unaware that the safety chute was out. The "City of Salt Lake" was using a new parachute for the record runs.

"Awfully disappointed" about the crash, Zeldine Graham said she would delay her decision about rebuilding the car for a few weeks. "I'm just not thinking right now."

Early in November she reached her decision. She said she would try again in 1964.

Why?

"To try and retrieve some of the money I've spent on it. I don't know what it will mean by way of money if we can beat the mark. But it should bring some of it back.

"It will take money. Unless we can find someone to help by way of parts, it will be my expense. Two of the tires are gone. We figured that some piece of wire cut up one of the tires on the last run and caused our defeat. Another was also cut. Where the wire came from I don't know.

"We may get some financial help on the body. Otherwise, we don't have much to do to put the

The "Wingfoot Express" used 15 rockets for propulsion. *Courtesy Goodyear Tire and Rubber Company.*

127

racer back on the run. We expect to have it ready to go in the spring.''

There was considerable opposition to her plans to rebuild the car. People feared someone else might be killed in it.

"We have thought about it a long time," she replied. "But we'll try again. We came so close last time."

But when the gallant widow failed to gain financial backing, she reluctantly gave up the fight.

Dr. Nathan Ostich was back at the Flats in September, 1963, with a modified jet.

The suspension, made up of modified standard trunk parts, was junked and replaced with aircraft components. The steering wheel ratio was slowed for better high speed control and a new steering shock absorption unit added to front steering arms. In addition, tires on the streamliner were modified to provide more tread and traction.

It had been reported that the project cost Ostich more than $100,000 and involved 10,000 man hours. The doctor would not confirm this.

Despite the changes, Ostich's luck didn't change.

On September 21, the "Flying Caduceus" spun out of control during a practice run. Moments before, Ostich had been clocked at 322 and was slowing down when the machine began to spin. His estimated speed at the time was 75 miles an hour.

Members of the crew said Ostich apparently applied the brakes too hard. Damage was minor.

"Gee, I didn't realize it was so slippery down there," said Ostich as he climbed from the car.

On September 27, 1963, Ostich made runs of 354 and 351 miles an hour as the "Caduceus" showed symptoms of engine trouble. Two days later the dejected doctor called off further land-speed attempts after a 359 clocking.

"The experts have done all they can here. We just can't get that crucial last 10 percent of power."

It was the last ride for Nathan Ostich.

Maybe Ostich thought it was time to leave the daredevil driving to the youngsters. After all, he was 55 years old.

To build a faster jet-car would take more capital, and the California doctor had spent an estimated $100,000 in his pursuit of the land speed record.

It had become too obvious after repeated efforts that his "Flying Caduceus" would not crack the 400 mile an hour barrier. The options were clear: start from scratch or reluctantly retire.

Dr. Nathan Ostich did the latter.

13
Duel on the Salt

The great jet duel took place at Bonneville between October 1964 and November of 1965. During that period, eight records were set, with the speed increased from 407 to 600 miles an hour.

In 1964, the record changed hands no less than five times. Art Arfons and his "Green Monster" were declared the winners with a two-way average of 536.75.

That speed season began with the record at 407.45. And what a season!

First, Tom Green powered Walt Arfons' "Wingfoot Express" to a new two-way mark of 413.02 on bursts of 405.55 and 420.07. Three days later—October 5—Art Arfons gunned his jet to an unlimited record of 434.02, including a blistering last run of 479.62.

Next it was Craig Breedlove's turn on the salt, and the Californian increased the record to 468.719. That was on October 13. Forty-eight hours later, Breedlove became the first man to shatter the 500-mile-an-hour barrier. He stormed through the flying mile at a 526.277 clip, and survived a scary, runaway ride on the return trip. By the time Breedlove finally stopped his "Spirit" of America," the three-wheeler had sailed six miles off course and rolled into a canal. Breedlove was finished for the year.

Twelve days after the crash, Art Arfons returned to the Flats to regain his record. He was to remain the fastest man on wheels until Breedlove could renew the fight with a more powerful weapon.

For the second consecutive year, it appeared that Walt Arfons would return to Akron, Ohio emptyhanded.

In 1963, the Arfons-Green team was stopped dead in its tracks by wet salt which flew into the 8,000-horsepower jet engine, bringing the "Wingfoot Express" to a halt after four runs. The car had turned in a smooth 250 run when trouble developed.

To prevent a similar occurence, deflectors were added to keep salt away from the engine. In addition, fins were put to the front for stability and steering.

Arfons was confident his 8,000-horsepower creation could snare the record. "I know the 'Wingfoot' is capable of 500 miles an hour, but I'll be satisfied with 450." He was jubilant to reach 413.02.

The record came with less than an hour of sunlight left. If unsuccessful, they would have had to wait two weeks until Art Arfons and Breedlove took their turns on the Flats.

Trouble developed early in the week.

"Even when I made my first run," recalls Green, "I was getting pressure in the cockpit. There was indication around the windshield. Too much pressure would have ripped off the seven-foot plexiglas cockpit canopy.

"There was also engine pulsating the first day. The whole car felt like it was shaking. There was also power surging. I just couldn't control the car. It would have sluggish movement, then unexpectedly start surging.

"Walt thought the engine was bad, so we replaced it with a spare. We finally tried the new engine but it wasn't running right. Things were looking plain miserable."

Top speed through the frustrating week was 299 miles an hour.

Arriving early at Bonneville, Art Arfons

watched. Although he and his brother had workshops just a few yards apart and lived near each other, they hadn't spoken since 1959. Years before they had built a string of record-setting "Green Monsters" that dominated the drag strips.

Each had a different reason for the rift.

"I wanted to build a jet car and Arthur wanted to stay with the piston," said Walter. "But people wanted to see something different. So I built a jet and started making money and bookings like crazy. Two years later (1961) Arthur built his jet 'Cyclops'—my brother's a hard man to work with."

Art had another version.

"In 1956 Walt decided to quit racing because there was no money in it. So Ed Snyder and I built 'Green Monster No. 11' that set all those national hot rod records in 1957-58-59.

"Walt then built his first car alone in 1959 and it didn't run. He was mad because his car didn't run. In 1962 we dissolved our partnership in the feed mill."

Walt Arfons drove his "Green Monster," the world's first jet dragster, more than 600 times at speeds exceeding 200 miles an hour.

Walt's closest call came when the "Monster" sliced through a cyclone fence, jumped two ditches, crossed a highway and wound up 75 feet in the woods. Fortunately, he was just shaken up. The drag strip accident was triggered by parachute failure. It seemed the speed was beyond the design load of the chutes. The two safety cutes ripped from the car when Arfons pulled the release switch.

His top speed in the quarter-mile was 242, set at Miami, Florida in 1961. Walt had hoped to set the world land speed record himself, but a mild heart condition developed and ended his racing days.

He and Tom Green, a sales manager for a Wheaton, Illinois tool company, conceived the idea for the jet racer in early 1962. Arfons built the frame and mounted the surplus J-46 engine. Then the car was transported to Green's garage and the complete body fitted. It flopped in 1963 and appeared headed for the same fate when Art Arfons offered Green a bit of advice which turned the trick. At a press conference following his record, Green called the tip a "significant contribution." The difference between 299 and a 413 average was the widening of the exhaust cone opening from 17 to 19 inches.

"At 17 inches," explained Green, the engine pressure became too great and a fuel-metering system automatically cut off the fuel supply."

Although the engine lost horsepower with the bigger cone it functioned properly for the first time.

"By Friday morning (October 2), we had an engine we could trust, even though the horsepower had been reduced. Walt then decided to try the afterburner which I had never tried before."

Green was apprehensive. Before he stepped into the cockpit of the "Wingfoot Express," the self-taught aerodynamics expert had never driven a race car.

Giving the burner three short bursts, Green averaged 406.

On his return run, the 31-year-old driver pulled the afterburner lever one-half mile from the timing clocks, "but it didn't hit hard at all. I just kept the lever down through the mile.

"The needle vibrated at 400 miles per hour and I thought we missed the record. I was tickled pink to find out the car averaged 420 on the final run. Going 400 miles an hour is quite a thrill, like falling through the sky."

Walt Arfons was elated. "The car held the ground beautifully," he said. Records show the "Wingfoot Express" made 14 futile runs before it suddenly sprang to life.

Little did Arfons and Green realize their hard-earned triumph would last for only 72 hours. It was an indication of things to come.

Art Arfons wasn't a patient man.

On October 4, he made a gingerly trip of 350. "The car felt good and I was using only half power." The following day was also scheduled for practice. Records don't usually come quickly in an untested car. He clocked a respectable 396.34. When the speed came so easily, Arfons decided to go all-out for the record. His run was a blistering 479.62 for a new two-way record of 434.20.

"I honestly had no intention of attempting the record," he explained. "I was just going out the first time and try for the 375 mark. The car felt so good that I nudged it up and hit 401 (in the kilometer)."

Arfons needed a clocking of 438 on the return trip to cement the record.

"I felt this was as good a time as any. I turned it loose and went but I didn't use all the power. In fact, I didn't turn on the afterburner. It was a tremendous sensation. Everything went by so fast that it was over almost before I got started good."

Firestone racing engineers estimated Arfons used 10,000 of the potential 17,500 horsepower on the 479 run. "With a few adjustments," he said, "I think the car is capable of breaking 500 without a lot of trouble"

Two days later, Art took dead aim at the 500 barrier.

The needle was touching 500 when a three-inch bolt, imbedded under the earth's crust, was forced loose by the power of the "Monster" and slammed against the right rear tire and back panel. Fortunately he was able to bring the homemade car to a halt some 2½ miles after the blowout. Arfons was temporarily out of action.

"I would have had a 530 run," he commented.

That gave Breedlove the opening he needed, and the 26-year-old ex-hot rodder took advantage. On October 13, he piloted the "Spirit of America" to a new record of 468. The runs: 442.59 and 498.13. At 468, it took him about 8 seconds to go through the measured mile. Forty-two minutes later the car was turned around for the return run.

What did he do while the car was refueled, the chutes repacked?

"I just walked around. I was kind of nervous. I checked the throttle setting, and then just walked around. I usually just kick salt."

Two days later, Breedlove climbed back into the cockpit. He wanted to put the world land speed record beyond the reach of Arfons' powerful jet. He upped the mark to 526.26, crashing into a canal.

"My wife wants me to quit, but I don't think it'll be too tough getting her to change her mind. There's not too much money in this business, but there's a tremendous personal satisfaction in being the first to hit 500. That's like hitting 60 home runs in baseball or the way the four-minute mile used to be in track and field."

Breedlove showed no signs of remorse when Arfons upped the record to 536.75 on October 27. "Boy, isn't that something," he remarked.

A high-speed blowout on the return run silenced the screaming "Monster." Opening the throttle on the return run (Art had previously clocked 515.98), Arfons cut loose the afterburner. The right rear tire blew and he took a death grip on the steering wheel. Art pressed the chute-eject button, but the chute blew away. The hydraulic pressure gauge read zero—no brakes.

Then a new danger developed. His right front tire was rubbing against the "Monster's" frame

and was burning. Smoke filled the cockpit, and Arfons began choking. Quickly he unlatched the canopy and slowly, fresh air mingled with the nauseating smoke.

Now the "Monster" was cutting huge "S's" in the salt. Finally, the indicator plummeted to 185, 150, then 100. With a mile of usable salt remaining, Arfons knew he was out of danger.

Speed for the scary ride was 559.19.

"My biggest mistake," he said following the run, "was going too darn fast. The tires did a great job. I had agreed not to run over 550 on the air-speed indicator but my foot just got too darn heavy. I figured something would go—but I wanted the record.

"The car handled beautifully. I'd like to try 600 next. The sound barrier will present a big problem after that, but I know the car will go over 650."

How did Arfons feel during the runs?

"It scared the hell out of me. The rough salt bounced me around but it was worth the bouncing."

Even after the record had been boosted to 536.75, Walt Arfons wasn't through. If his "Wingfoot Express" didn't have the power to get the job done, he intended to experiment with JATO (jet assist take-off) rockets. His plan was to place one rocket in back of the cockpit and two at the rear of the cigar-shaped racer. However, both FIA and USAC refused to sanction the rockets.

It marked the second time that the governing bodies of racing had turned down a request to use rockets as a power booster. When Mickey Thompson brought his four-engine "Challenger I" to the Flats several years previous, he also had a supply of JATO bombs. The United States Auto Club ruled: "A car shall be moved only by its own power during a record attempt." The FIA said it "will study applications for recognition of records made or beaten by other manned vehicles than those corresponding to the definition of the word 'automobile' as it appears in the international sporting code. These vehicles will have to run only on the surface of the ground on at least four wheels, two of which must be steering wheels. The propellent will possibly be assured by other means than the wheels, but propelling and steering will, however, have to be completely controlled by a person on board the car."

However, the driver of the "Wingfoot Express," Bob Tatroe, did not control the rockets. He activated a switch which unleashed the three rockets. But once activated, he could not control the amount of thrust or shut them off.

If a car could be built which employed rockets as the primary source of power, and if the driver could control that power, USAC said it would consider such a type vehicle as a candidate for the unlimited thrust record.

It would be a year before Walt Arfons returned to Bonneville with his all-new rocket-propelled "Wingfoot Express."

In the meantime, he had to settle for the woman's land speed record. Returning to the Flats in November of 1964, he not only brought with him his record-setting "Wingfoot" but "The Avenger," a jet dragster.

Mrs. Paula Murphy, a 29-year-old mother from San Fernando Valley, California, drove "Avenger" to a new woman's mark of 226.37, breaking her old record of 161.20 set in a piston-powered car.

That record would later be broken, first by Betty Skelton in Art Arfons' jet dragster, "Cyclops," and then by Lee Breedlove in her husband's "Spirit of America-Sonic I."

14
Another Barrier Falls

Art Arfons was back at the Flats in 1965 to defend his land-speed title against two adversaries, each with a different look.

Craig Breedlove challenged with the "Spirit of America-Sonic I," a jet with twice the power of his badly damaged three-wheeler. The new bottle-shaped car boasted 15,000 horsepower from its J-79 with three-stage afterburner.

Turning to a new source of propulsion, Walt Arfons had designed and built a massive five-ton "Wingfoot Express" which looked like an Atlas missile. Bob Tatroe, who drove one of Arfons' jet dragsters, was picked to handle the rocket racer.

Walt oozed confidence when he discussed the upcoming speed season. In the span of 23 seconds, he said, the rocket-propelled Wingfoot would unleash its full 28,000 horsepower kick to demolish the existing land-speed record by some 200 miles an hour! Tatroe would release the rockets every two seconds. Five bursts and 17.8 seconds later, the "Wingfoot Express" would enter the measured mile at 714.

"Midway through the run the 'Wingfoot' will be hitting 750. The run through the mile should last 4.87 seconds. That's 739 miles per hour. And at 4.9 seconds, the speed would be 726."

Before the all-out speed attempt, Arfons explained, "we'll make a run into the 300s, a run into the 400s, followed by several at 600.

"Since nobody knows what happens when a car approaches sound-barrier speed, we'll work up to that gradually. By the end of the first week, Bob will nudge 700 if the shock waves aren't too great. Then in October we'll shoot for the barrier."

On September 15, 1965, the world's first rocket-powered land-speed racer made a publicity run down Akron-Canton Airport runway.

Spurting orange and lavender flames and blanketing the runway with billowing smoke, the car reached an estimated speed of 120—propelled by two of its 15 JATO rockets.

Dimensions of the car were: length, 28 feet; wheelbase, 15 feet, 5 inches; height, 9 feet to top of fin; ground clearance, 15 inches; width, 12 feet, 6 inches; frame, steel; body covering, tempered aluminum (fiberglass nose).

The 35-inch tires had been specially designed by Goodyear engineers to operate at supersonic speeds. The company also designed wheels, brakes and braking parachutes.

Although the car had four wheels, it had a definite triangular appearance. The two front wheels were set close together, the fender-covered rear wheels 13 feet apart.

The massive car, steered through the front wheels and a canard fin on its nose, was "tailor-made" for Tatroe. The cockpit was built with the interior shaped to his dimensions. Even the seat was form-fitted.

Walt Arfons figured the unlimited land-speed record would come easy. He was dead wrong.

First on the Flats, the "Wingfoot Express" unleashed all 15 rockets, but managed an average of only 247.59 from a standing start. Speed for the last 2,000 feet of the mile: 406.40.

Tatroe said the air-speed indicator read 485 at one point.

Disappointed but not downhearted, Arfons said he'd be back at Bonneville with more rockets.

"We'll break the sound barrier yet," he vowed.

Rocket-powered "Wingfoot Express" being built in Walt Arfons' shop.

"Wingfoot Express" being built.

Rear-end view of car, where 15 rockets are fitted.

"Wingfoot Express."

"But remember, this is the first rocket-powered car, and you've got to move slowly and check things out."

Although Art Arfons was not scheduled for the salt until October 24, he couldn't resist the temptation of setting the quarter-mile acceleration record from a standing start. A special portion of the track was prepared for the attempt. On September 29, the Ohio hot-rodder applied full power to the 17,500-horsepower "Green Monster" and blazed to a speed of 258.62 for the 1320 foot run.

The run, timed by the American Hot Rod Association and certified by USAC, was over in 6.9 seconds. It marked the first time Arfons had ever applied full power to his 21-foot jet car.

Art emerged from his tiny cockpit with a wide smile.

"Well, I'm not worried now," he said. "I just never knew how the engine would react when the full juice was on. It ran smooth as silk."

The run was one of the most spectacular ever witnessed on the historic race course. A sheet of flame over 100 feet long shot out of the massive J-79 engine all the way down the course.

Arfons, who spent 10 years on the nation's drag strips before breaking the land speed record, said the quarter-mile drag record was the most significant thing he had accomplished in racing outside of the unlimited thrust mark.

"This meant an awful lot to me because I was brought up on the drag strips. Everyone has said that you couldn't run over 250 no matter what power you had because of the short space. Actually, it surprised me a little when they told me the time."

So Art packed up his "Green Monster" and headed back to Akron—and waited. "I can't predict what Breedlove or Tatroe will do but we'll be prepared to go back immediately if they break our record."

By October 12, Breedlove and his "Spirit of America-Sonic I" were ready to make their move. Dimensions of the car: length, 34 feet, 7 inches; width, 7 feet, 1 inch; height, top of tail fin, 10 feet, 6 inches; wheel base, 202 inches; weight, dry, 8,000 pounds; frame, welded tubular construction of chrome molybdenum steel body panels, aluminum and fiberglass construction; steering

"Wingfoot Express." Bob Tatroe in cockpit. Walt Arfons standing. *Courtesy Goodyear Tire & Rubber Company.*

front wheels only. Unlike his first land speed creation, "Sonic I" had four wheels.

Breedlove was sure he and his 15,000 horsepower jet had regained the record, but official clocking told a different story—516.203.

The Californian was irate. "It can't be," he snapped. "There's something wrong with the timing lights. I used a higher power setting on the second and third runs but went slower. I can't explain it." His best speed for three runs through the traps was 518.769.

In addition to the lack of power, he was faced with another problem. The "Spirit" suffered heavy body stress during the three runs. The nose section caved in and the top body panel was wrinkled by wind damage.

While Breedlove and his crew returned to nearby Wendover to repair the car, Walt Arfons and his rocket car were ready for the second Bonneville appearance within two weeks.

After a delay caused by heavy rain, the "Wingfoot Express" roared off the launching pad. Its speed was a disappointing 438.66. During the run, one of the 25 JATO rockets fell off the car and another fired the wrong way. As a result, some of the metal skin, wiring and part of the firewall protecting Bob Tatroe were singed by the heat.

Tatroe fired in two bursts, exploding 15 rockets and then following up with 10 more rockets to sustain speed through the mile. His peak speed through the mile was 580.

Although Arfons said his "Wingfoot Express" could be repaired for another run in early November, he beat that timetable by one week. The rocket racer would make one more try for the record in 1965.

In the meantime, Breedlove was back in action with the mystery of the power loss solved.

"What happened was my motor back fired," he explained. "We call it decel stall. That means t de-accelerated while under full power."

On October 20, he gave it the gun and nearly lost his life when the front wheels became airborne at 600 miles an hour.

With Breedlove checking over the slightly damaged "Spirit," Walt Arfons came back for another attempt. It wasn't enough; Tatroe averaged 470.53. It was apparent that two major problems had not been solved—the proper sequence of firing and the approach before entering the measured mile.

Despite its inability to capture the unlimited thrust record, the "Wingfoot Express" had ushered in the rocket age. But that would have to wait a few years.

In the meantime, Craig Breedlove and Art Arfons would continue their jet duel.

Following Breedlove's 600 runaway, two wings about two feet long were added to the front of the car to force the nose down. On November 2, he powered the "Spirit of America-Sonic I" to a speed of 544.382 on its first run through the meas-

Tom Green, driver of "Wingfoot Express," gets instructions
from Walt Arfons. Car set land-speed mark of 413 mph.
Courtesy Goodyear Tire and Rubber Company.

Cockpit of "Wingfoot Express." Note indicator near 700
mph.

"Wingfoot Express" during record run. *Courtesy Goodyear
Tire and Rubber Company.*

"Wingfoot Express" during record run. *Courtesy Goodyear Tire and Rubber Company.*

ured mile. On the return trip, the "Spirit" accelerated to 566.394 for a new two-way mark of 555.127 miles per hour. It was his fourth land speed record since 1963.

Breedlove had only one anxious moment, when his braking chute didn't open. He had to use the emergency parachute to slow down on the second run.

"I never had to work so hard for a record in my life. The car accelerated well and it was pretty smooth at 500 miles an hour. The track is drying out and was kind of like a washboard at the start."

Instead of leaving the Flats, Craig decided to wait around for Art Arfons. He knew the dogged determination of his rival.

Five days later—November 7—Arfons regained his record with a two-way speed of 576.533 on bursts of 575.724 and 577.386.

Arfons had hoped to be the first to crack the 500 mile an hour barrier. Breedlove beat him to the punch. He wanted to be the first to better 600 on land. However, he blew a tire on the second run. The "Green Monster" careened into a course marker and suffered extensive damage.

Art had to return to Ohio to repair the car and hope that Breedlove would fail. On November 15, 1965, Breedlove not only regained the record but averaged 600.601.

The salt was soggy as "Spirit" streaked across the Flats at 593.178. Using all three stages of afterburner, Breedlove steered the jet car to an even faster clocking of 608.201 on the return trip. On this historic 608 trip, the car veered to the left after leaving the measured mile and there was momentary fear that Breedlove was in trouble. However, the chute opened and Craig stopped the 34-footer beside his trailer-van headquarters.

"I wanted to park my car right in the garage," he laughed.

With Arfons' car out of action and winter moving in over the western Utah speedway, USAC officials called it quits for the year.

15

The Wildest Ride

In November of 1966, a big bus headed westward with a man and his hopes. Art Arfons was determined to regain his world land speed record.

Three months earlier, Arfons and his "Green Monster," along with a team of Firestone engineers, were at the Flats to conduct a series of tests. They wanted to find out why the right rear tire had exploded in 1964 and 1965. Delicate instruments were rigged to the "Monster" to record tire load at various speeds.

It was determined that the sudden torque applied when Arfons kicked in the four-stage afterburner placed a sharp load on the right rear tire. The afterburner adds raw jet fuel into the airstream, thereby increasing the engine's thrust by as much as 50 percent.

Firestone had tested the tires for 50 seconds at 650 miles per hour with a 2,000 pound load. The results at the Flats were startling.

"I knew there had to be an overload on the right rear tire, but I had no idea it was 6,000 pounds," said Arfons.

The scientific findings necessitated several changes in the jet car. Arfons added a small wing or airfoil at the rear end of the "Monster" to lift 3000 pounds of load off the car. The angle of the tailpipe was changed to create lift from the exhaust. Dual tires were added.

In addition, Arfons modified his specially-designed air intake probe. This bulb-shaped probe served two functions. First, it controlled the flow of air into the jet engine, thereby preventing any sputtering or choking of the massive powerplant. Second, it was to provide Arfons with data on his sound barrier attempt. On such a run, the probe would penetrate the powerful shock waves created by faster-than sound speed.

He came up with the radical idea after visiting Bunker Hill Air Force Base, which designed this probe for its B-58 bombers, the only planes in the world that hit barrier speeds at low altitudes.

During the September experimentation, the "Green Monster" clocked speeds of 450. Arfons was confident the overload problem had been licked. He didn't want to ride out another scare—another 600 mile-an-hour blowout.

"The first run," he recalled, "was great, despite the bumpy track. I nosed the car up and held my speed between 560 and 590. I only went into minimum burner." The speed: 575.724.

Forty-minutes later the two braking chutes were repacked and Arfons was ready for the all-important return run.

"I hit the timing clocks at over 500. The air speed indicator jumped and kept going until it was up to about 625. I was only in the mile about six seconds. I was at the end of the clocks and pushed down harder."

Then it happened.

"The right rear tire blew and I started leaving the track. Then smoke poured into the cockpit and I lost sight of the guide line for a moment. That's when I began to feel uneasy.

"For a moment I couldn't see a thing. Suddenly everything cleared. I gripped the steering wheel tight and tried to straighten it out, but before I could I crashed into the metal marker.

"Pieces started flying, including my canopy. I finally stopped, got out and looked at the car. It was a mess, but I knew I had the record."

Asked how he felt, Arfons said:

"I feel fine, but I broke my car."

The frame was broken in four places. The entire right side was mangled. The left side looked like swiss cheese after ramming into the steel marker.

But that was in November of 1965. Now it was one year later. The car was fixed like new.

Arfons made his first Bonneville appearance on November 14, 1966. His first run was a warmup—376.254—followed by a faster 474.934 clocking. Now he was ready for a record assault.

At 6:05 p.m., Arfons and his new-look "Monster" were poised 2½ miles from the measured mile.

"The car accelerated so quickly it jumped my foot off the gas pedal. When I got back and hit the burner, it didn't light at first. Then it caught, but too late," Arfons explained after his 544.017 run.

But by then it was too dark. Sunset had closed in on the Flats.

It had been a frustrating day. While the bottom wing, cocked exhaust and dual tires had taken the load off the 7,800 pound jet car, Arfons had trouble with the braking chutes. Both parachutes failed to open on the first run. On the second, a premature release required almost three hours of painstaking handstitching to repair the shredded nylon chute. The same right chute was charred by the full blast of the "Green Monster's" afterburner during Arfons' third solo. However, he considered the trouble to be minor. All it required was tracing the wiring to find the short. He had three safety chutes available instead of four.

It was an omen of things to come.

In the past, the world land speed record had come easily to the Ohioan. Now it had become hard and frustrating work for the three-time speed king. In two days Arfons had squeezed himself in the cockpit six times.

He made three more runs on November 15. The first, a warmup of 436.07, was designed to set the stage for faster clockings.

Arfons went faster, but 524.936 and 541.924 salvos weren't fast enough. The 524 trim was made with little help from the four-stage afterburner, which lit momentarily, went out, then sputtered and died.

"I was getting fuel but I wasn't getting any burner," said a dejected and puzzled Arfons.

In his 541 burst, "I just ran out of power and shut down in the middle of the run."

Arfons and his crew spent the remainder of the day trying to solve the perplexing problem. It was finally determined that a clogged fuel line had caused the afterburner's failure. The line was cleaned and the car readied for the next day. However, wind gusts up to 17 miles an hour postponed any runs on November 16.

On Thursday, November 17, a grim-faced Art Arfons stepped into the cockpit. "I'm going to stand on the accelerator clear through the mile," he said, softly but firmly.

The "Green Monster" whined and shrieked as it headed for the measured mile, some two miles away. A brilliant trail of orange flame followed the jet car as it raced out of sight.

Shortly after streaking past the final timing lights, the "Monster" veered to the left of the black line. Trying to get back on course, Arfons pulled the steering wheel hard right. The car pitched violently on its right side, then hit nose first. It became airborne at least twice and skidded for long distances on its right side.

When it finally settled on its belly, the "Monster" was almost one mile past the traps and some 100 yards off course.

Parts of the once-proud jet racer were strewn all over the Flats. Huge chunks were torn out of the salt, some as deep as 12 inches. The left cockpit was splattered with blood, the instrument panel smashed. The famed Green Monster lay hammered into an unbelieveable pile of junk. Now the car Arfons affectionately called "my baby" was silent.

His face covered with blood, the three-time speed king was hurriedly removed from the battered left cockpit and placed on a waiting private plane for the 125-mile flight from Bonneville to Salt Lake City.

All during the flight, Arfons kept asking about the car: "Can it be repaired?"

About two hours later, the report came over the State Patrol car radio at the Flats. Arfons was okay. No broken bones. He suffered salt burns and cuts from flying glass. His body ached all over.

Just a few visitors were allowed in Room 464. One visitor was Art's brother and one-time rival, Walt, who flew from Akron to Salt Lake City.

Although his eyes were covered with gauze and the skin around his eyes and cheekbones was raw, Art Arfons tried to joke. When he asked the nurse for toothbrush and toothpaste, the nurse asked: "What brand?"

"Gleem, naturally," he wise-cracked. "It has 93 percent fewer cavities.

Although still under sedation, Arfons talked about the crash and how he managed to survive.

"I couldn't really tell what happened. I suddenly noticed I was left of the black line, tried to control it and lost control. When the 'Green Monster' flipped the first time I didn't know it was gone. It got up and was coming in to crash a second time when I blacked out. When I came to in the plane I could feel my toes and fingers and said to myself, 'Boy, I'm all together.'"

How did Arfons survive the 600 mile an hour crash?

"I was wearing my lucky jacket," he quipped.

The well-worn black leather jacket had been his constant racing companion since 1957. In fact, Arfons repaired a torn portion of the jacket with an ancient foot-pedal sewing machine one day before he left for the Flats.

Twenty-four hours after he miraculously escaped death, Art Arfons flew home to recuperate and begin thinking about a new and faster "Monster." It was just what his older brother had predicted at the Salt Lake hospital.

"Racing is his life," philosophized Walt. "Arthur's let the quest of speed possess him. He has to be on top and he won't stop until he gets there, is mangled or killed. He certainly was fortunate. Someone had to be riding with him."

It wasn't until the "Green Monster" was back in Akron, Ohio that Art was able to reconstruct what happened:

"When the car started sliding on its right side, it threw a tremendous load on the right front corner. That overheated and froze the bearing on the spindle and burnt it right off. The wheel dug in and she went."

Entering the measured mile on second-stage afterburner, Arfons was officially clocked at 585. Leaving, the speedometer showed 610.

"Boy she really accelerated," he beamed.

Arfons credited fast work by his crew for saving his life.

"The fuel tank had split and I was doused with fuel, and with the intense heat of the engine (3,000 degrees), it was just a matter of time—maybe seconds—before the whole thing would have caught fire. But the crew was there and spraying chemical on the car before anything happened."

Art was amazed by all the letters and telegrams he received during the first weeks following the crash.

"It must be 200 by now and most of the mail is from people I don't even know. They're mostly concerned about my health."

Best wishes came from as far off as Brazil and Czechoslovakia.

His health was fine. He was sore all over.

"The black and blue is gone. So is the green," he laughed. "Now I'm turning yellow."

Arfons got the biggest chuckle out of a short note from a little girl. It read: "I hear you had clutch trouble. Put it together right."

16
Like Father, Like Son

Donald Campbell was born to set speed records. He died in that lonely pursuit on a lake in England on January 4, 1967.

He was only 200 yards and one second from setting a world water speed record of 300 miles an hour when his jet-boat "Bluebird" leapt 50 feet into the air, looped backwards and crashed into Lake Coniston.

Campbell had blasted through the measured mile at a speed of 296 on his first run. All he needed was a return of 257 to exceed his existing mark of 276.33 miles an hour.

But Campbell wasn't the kind to play it safe. He was fearful of an American challenge and wanted to put the record out of reach.

When asked why he risked his life attempting to break records, he would simply reply: "We are doing this for Great Britain, old boy. Anybody who thinks there's money in it these days can have my bills."

It was shortly before 9 a.m. when the fatal run began. In bitterly cold weather, spectators stood on the water's edge, straining their eyes to pick out "Bluebird."

Campbell put his foot hard down to accelerate the massive jet boat to peak power. All appeared well. Suddenly his voice came excitedly over the radio from the cockpit of "Bluebird."

"Nose up...pitching a bit down here...probably from my own wash...straightening up now in my track...passing close to Peel Island...tramping like hell here...I can't see much over the top...I'm getting a lot of bloody row here...I can't see anything...I've got the bows up...I've gone...Oh..."

Campbell's estimated speed at the time of his tragic accident was 310.

The next day, Royal Navy frogman searched Lake Coniston. They found the main hull at a depth of 140 feet, Campbell's steering wheel, seat belt and even his good luck charm—Mr. Woppit, a teddy bear. However, Campbell's body was never found.

"I'm certain he was going to beat the 300 mark," said racing official Norman Buckley. "He would not have gone on with the boat any further. He thought that 300 was her limit. Anything over his last record was going into the unknown, and this is a task he accepted."

What could have caused the accident? Buckley didn't know.

"The conditions were as perfect as I have ever seen...In another few yards he would have been safe and would have broken the record."

Campbell knew the risk involved in pushing the ancient "Bluebird." He knew that anything exceeding the critical three degrees of uplift on her nose would result in disaster. Over and over he had watched the newsreel of John Cobb crashing to his death on Loch Ness in 1952.

"I have seen the film of that terrible moment hundreds and hundreds of times," he once said. "We have drawn up a graph six feet long showing all the forces of air and water that must have acted on Cobb's boat."

He described in detail how the film showed a dark shape hurtling and skimming along the water ahead of the boat. "That was Cobb...that could happen to me."

Thus the legend of the racing Campbells was

over. Together, father and son established 21 land and water-speed records during a period that covered more than four decades.

While Donald was best known for his records on water, he smashed the land speed record for wheel-driven cars in 1964, thus becoming the first man to set both land and water records the same year.

To Campbell's friends, it seemed his whole purpose in life was to outdo the achievements of his famous father, Sir Malcolm, the speed king of the 1920s and 30s.

Sir Malcolm, who set nine land and four water marks, would never permit his son to enter the record-breaking game. He used to say: "I must be the first and last racing man in the family." But within a few weeks of Sir Malcolm's death in 1948, Campbell launched his own speed career.

As a boy, Campbell once said he regarded his father as a god—"and a very changeable, inscrutable god at that. Father was such a dominating character in that no one living as close to him as I

Donald Campbell in 1961. *Courtesy Deseret News*.

did could possibly have accepted everything he did and said without being driven into the ground. Sometimes I worshipped him. Sometimes I kicked against him very hard."

The influence of his father haunted Campbell, perhaps even more after Sir Malcolm died. Intensely superstitious and holding strong convictions of life-after-death, Donald Campbell was convinced that his father's spirit was always with him. He believed that they were frequently in direct spiritual communication.

He was convinced that on several occasions his father's intervention had saved him from disaster. The first time was at Lake Coniston in 1957, just before he raised the water speed record to 239.07. A medium at a seance had warned him of unspecified danger. Campbell believed the message originated from his father and ordered a complete overhaul of "Bluebird" before he made his run.

The second occasion was also at Coniston, a year later, when the steering failed and Campbell found himself heading for a pier at high speed.

"Suddenly the throttle opened wide, the launch answered to the helm and we were clear of danger. Again I knew someone else had acted for me."

He also believed his father was with him in 1960 when his jet-powered "Bluebird" crashed at 360 at the Bonneville Salt Flats.

After the car had somersaulted three times and bounced along on its side for 1¼ miles, Campbell got out and walked to an ambulance. He escaped with a hairline skull fracture. Later, Campbell told a friend that his father's face appeared at the windshield during the crash and said, "Don't worry, Donald. You'll be all right.

Some friends believed his character changed after that. The possibility of another crash became an obsession with him. Others questioned his courage. They wondered whether he could ever push a car or a boat to the limit.

Despite his superstitions, Campbell showed the doubters and the world his courage.

Three years after his spectacular crash, Campbell took dead aim on the land speed record. But the relentless rains at Lake Eyre in Australia stymied his bid.

Yet, always the sportsman, Campbell called it a "jolly good effort" when Craig Breedlove shattered John Cobb's long-standing record in August of that year. Breedlove blazed across Bonneville at a 407 clip.

Donald Campbell's "Bluebird after its 1960 crash at Bonneville Salt Flats. *Courtesy Deseret News*.

Donald Campbell with his wife Tonia and his mascot, Mr. Woppit. The stuffed animal was with Campbell during all his record attempts—on land and on water. *Courtesy Australian Information Service*.

Jet boat "Bluebird" lying off shore at Lake Dumbleyung, 160 miles south of Perth, West Australia. On Dec. 31, 1964, Donald Campbell set new water mark of 276.33 on Lake Dumblyung. *Courtesy Australian Information Service.*

Breedlove's car had three wheels instead of the conventional four. In addition, "Spirit of America' was propelled by pure thrust, rather than a piston engine that transmitted its power directly through the wheels.

"I don't think this is really important," commented Campbell. "Technically, yes. But in the eyes of the world, no. If we were to succeed in beating Cobb's record with 'Bluebird' and fail to break Breedlove's as well, then in my mind, we have failed."

Campbell had never been happy with the length of the Bonneville course—11 miles in 1960—because the placement of the measured mile at midpoint left little room for braking. He wanted a longer speedway and narrowed the choice to three sites—Lake Eyre, a dried-up salt lake in Australia, a site in the Caucasus Mountains and a site in the Trucial of Oman in the Persian Gulf area.

He ruled out the Trucial of Oman site because it could not be reached by road or rail. The site in the Caucasus was not suitable because it was in the USSR.

That left Lake Eyre, located 450 miles north of Adelaide, South Australia, an area which few white men had explored.

Several persons, including Campbell, went out to see the salt beds at first hand. Campbell even drove a Jaguar at more than 100 miles an hour across the salt, which was harder than Bonneville's. Then the team of British companies backing the venture weighed the first-hand evidence.

Campbell's backers decided that Lake Eyre would be the site for several reasons: a longer raceway, which meant that acceleration and braking could be more gradual, and better tire traction, because the salt-sand mixture was so hard and dry. In addition, the danger of crosswinds would be greatly reduced, provided the attempt was made in April or May, because studies conducted over a 30-year period showed the calmest conditions had been recorded then.

Campbell and his team felt they had the perfect speedway for the perfect car. Since the spectacular crash in 1960, the $5.5 million "Bluebird"—financed by 80 British firms—had been meticulously rebuilt and a lofty tail added for stability.

Its Proteus gas turbine aircraft engine produced

The late Donald Campbell of Great Britain. *Courtesy Mirror Australian Telegraph Publication.*

146

Technicians work on Donald Campbell's "Bluebird" at Lake Eyre. *Courtesy Advertiser Newspapers Ltd.*

4250 horsepower and its designers spoke of a 500 mile an hour potential, with 450 a realistic working goal. "It's hard to see," said co-designer Lewis Norris, "how any vehicle driven through the wheels can have a higher potential than this one. You can almost say this is the end of the road." But little did Norris, Campbell or any others involved in the project realize how difficult a job it would be. Heavy floods between mid-April and mid-May forced the "Bluebird" team to safety at Lake Eyre. On May 12, the sky was cloudy again but Campbell drove the jet-powered "Bluebird" at a respectable 240 miles an hour and said the car "behaved magnificently."

Six days later, however, he finally had to concede defeat. All Campbell could do was wait until 1964.

Despite the sad experience, it was decided to give Lake Eyre another try. But once again, the elements seemed to be working against the gutsy Englishman. For the first time in record, more than an inch of rain had fallen on Lake Eyre in May for two years in succession.

After almost three weeks of waiting, Campbell was ready for his first practice run. It was May 5, 1964. Although Campbell clocked 170 miles an hour, the salt was so soft that the four-ton "Bluebird" chopped ruts in the salt three inches deep. Campbell knew he couldn't make a record run under these circumstances. He searched hundreds of square miles of the lake, both by air and from the ground, for a harder running surface.

Campbell decided to try out a new track north of the existing course. With the aid of tractors pulling

"Bluebird." *Courtesy Advertiser Newspapers Ltd.*

steel girders, a new speedway was carved out.

The next step was to test the surface. Campbell gave the surface bursts up to 30 percent of full power. It was hard enough to warrant extending the track to 13 miles.

At least the track had been found, but now a new and hazardous problem developed. Hitting speeds of around 300, Campbell suddenly experienced violent vibrations. However, when the wheels and tires were changed, the vibrations stopped as suddenly as they had started. The solution had been found—or so it was thought. Salt sticking to the insides of the wheels had put them out of balance, so the wheels were to be thoroughly cleaned before each run.

Campbell's best clocking was a respectable 389 on July 1. Seven days later, Campbell announced that his present series of attempts would be post-

poned for the time being. The surface of the salt had become far too dangerous.

In mid-July, Campbell returned to Lake Eyre and said all he planned to make was four runs. Now all he needed was a dry surface and no wind.

On July 16, Campbell received word that Breedlove had announced intentions of returning to Bonneville in September to boost his record.

Campbell knew he had to act fast, but the following day was Friday and to a highly superstitious man Friday was the sign of the Black Cat.

It was a Friday in 1960 that Donald Campbell escaped death on another salt track thousands of miles away. But determined to duplicate the feat of his father as the fastest man on both land and water, Campbell pushed his fears aside for a run at the record.

It was Friday, July 17, 1964. The course was dry

Unusual shot of "Bluebird" being loaded onto trailer.
Courtesy Mirror Australian Telegraph Publications.

"Bluebird" streaks along the Lake Eyre speed track at 200 mph. *Courtesy Advertisers Newspapers Ltd.*

"Bluebird" in 1964 run. *Courtesy Mirror Australian Telegraph Publications.*

"Bluebird" at Lake Eyre, Australia, *Courtesy Mirror Australian Telegraph Publications*.

and the breezes subsided to a barely safe two miles an hour.

As Campbell was strapped in his cockpit, he said, "This is it, Friday be damned." He fired the jet engine and the "Bluebird" streaked across the salt. But immediately the car seemed to be weaving and cutting ruts in the surface. The right rear tire began throwing rubber. Somehow, Campbell held on and raced through the measured mile at 403.1 and 388.7 for the kilometer.

Almost an hour later, Campbell again fired up "Bluebird." The vibrations shook the car, but Campbell just gripped the steering wheel harder and managed to complete the run. Again his speed was 403.1. Speed through the kilometer was 400.5.

When Campbell stopped the car, the right rear tire tread was completely gone. Chunks of his

Dunlop tires were scattered over seven miles of the run. Again, he said, he saw visions of his father.

"I nearly killed myself. I was so near going out of control that it wasn't even funny. And when I was sitting in the cockpit at the end of the run I really thought I had had it. For I knew the second run would be worse. I saw no hope at all.

"It was then that it was so extraordinary. You know how the canopy lifts up with the windscreen in front of the cockpit? Well, I suddenly looked up into it and there was my father reflected in the windscreen. I even recognized the white shirt and flannels he used to wear.

"For a few seconds he just looked at me, smiling, then he said, 'Well boy. Now you know how I felt that time at Bonneville in 1935 when a front tire burst at 300. But don't worry. It'll be all right, boy.' Then he faded away."

Campbell's big disappointment was not traveling faster than Craig Breedlove. But he had smashed the record for wheel-driven cars.

Donald Campbell insisted that "Bluebird," in its present form, was still capable of reaching 450 miles an hour.

While he never had the chance to prove it, Campbell became the first man in the annals of speed to set both the land and water record during the same year.

In 1964, he gunned his jet-powered boat, "Bluebird," to a two-way water record of 260.32.

Before his death three years later, he was already working on plans for a rocket-propelled car to break the sound barrier.

As always, it was for the glory of England.

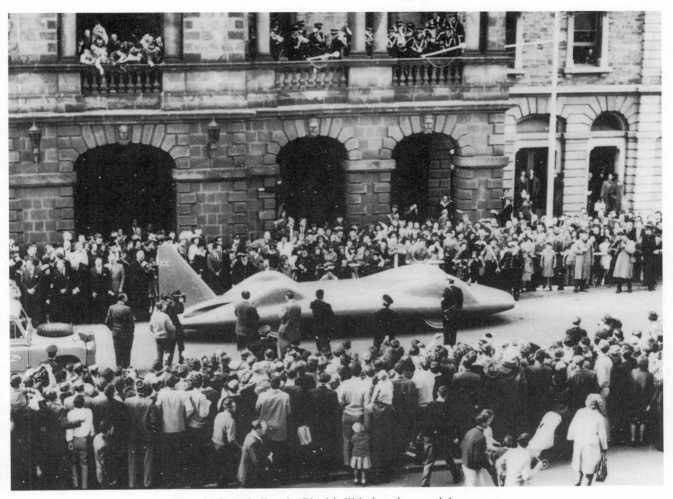

Donald Campbell and "Bluebird" being given a civic reception at the Town Hall of Adelaide on July 25, 1964, after breaking world land speed record. *Courtesy Advertiser Newspapers Ltd.*

17
The "Goldenrod"

Bobby Summers of Ontario, California is semi-retired, so to speak.

"Naturally, if someone breaks my record I'd be interested in racing again," declares the reigning land speed record holder for wheel-driven cars.

"I'd like to race, but we just can't drop our business unless it was worth a good amount of money."

On November 12, 1965, Summers drove his four-engine "Goldenrod" to a two-way average of 409.277 at Bonneville. It marked the first time since 1928 that an American held the axle-driven record (Ray Keech grabbed those honors). Summers' performance bettered the 403.1 set by the late Donald Campbell (July 17, 1964) at Lake Eyre in Australia.

Since then, only Mickey Thompson has taken a shot at the record.

"There's a lot of development left in 'Goldenrod,'" insists Summers. "It's really a relatively untested car with just 11 runs to its credit. There's much to be gained by engine development alone. I'm sure we could achieve 500 miles an hour, but not at Bonneville. There's just enough room for acceleration. I had about nine miles total and only four miles of approach which wasn't very much. All I could use were three of the four speeds."

He is confident the longest, narrowest package of piston power ever to snare the world land speed record could reach 500 miles an hour at a longer salt bed track such as Lake Eyre.

Since setting the record, Bobby and his brother, Bill, have devoted their energies to running their high performance equipment manufacturing business.

Although the owns the coveted record, Bobby

Summers realizes that most of the general public doesn't even know he exists.

"The public goes for big numbers," he sadly admits.

The public isn't really aware that there are two land speed classes. Jets and rocket racers are in the thrust unlimited class. Summers' "Goldenrod," on the other hand, is driven by four piston engines with the 2400 horsepower channeled directly through the wheels.

Men like Walt Arfons have high praise for the Californian. Arfons believes "a wheel-driven car presents tougher traction problems than a jet or rocket. You don't have to worry about getting the tires to bite. That's the big problem in a piston car. You need three things for a piston record—traction, perfect car construction and the perfect tire. First you have to apply the power easily. Don't and it's like driving on ice. Aerodynamics must be perfect because you won't be able to get all the horsepower out of the engine any other way. And of course you need a tire that will grip the salt."

That's fine praise indeed from a man who set an unlimited jet thrust record of 413.02 in 1964 and introduced rocketry to the land speed game one year later.

Bobby Summers was born April 4, 1937 in Omaha, Nebraska. As a child he and his brother, Bill, moved to California with their parents.

An industrial arts major in high school, Bobby spent most of his spare time around cars and hot rodding. His skills as a machinist and welder would serve him well in the major construction of the "Goldenrod."

From a Model A Ford which he acquired as a

Bob Summers (left) and his brother, Bill, builders of "Goldenrod." *Courtesy Chrysler Motor Company*.

youngster, Bob and Bill Summers collaborated on their first serious hot rod, a 1936 Ford with a Chrysler engine, which they ran at Bonneville in 1954.

With Bobby at the wheel, the Summers Brothers set a string of records at local drag strips, El Mirage Dry Lake and Bonneville. He joined the exclusive 200 hour club with a two-way clocking of 221.06 at Bonneville.

In 1962, at the Bonneville National Speed Trials, Summers drove their single-engine streamliner 322.79 miles an hour. The following year he established national and international Class C records with the same car. His speeds were 1 kilometer—283.71, 1 mile, 279.74.

Two years later, the handsome Californian smashed the land speed mark for axle-driven cars.

The "Goldenrod" was four years in the planning stage and took 53 weeks to build from the ground up.

By 1964 Bobby had quit his job as a mechanic. Bill was supporting both of them from his earnings

as a truck driver, so that his younger brother could devote full-time to launching the car's construction. They had a written presentation to solicit sponsorship for the "Goldenrod." Engineering studies had been made, a scale model built and some preliminary work on the car completed.

On paper the project appeared feasible, but it was totally impractical without major financial backing. For several months Bobby Summers made the rounds of potential sponsors. Just when it appeared that the project would have to be scrapped, George Hurst heard about it. Hurst, who sells many of his products to hot rodders, believed the car could be successful. He listened to the proposal and liked it, but time was running out. It was August of 1964 and unless the project was pushed to a full-time status at once, it would be too late to complete the car in time to run in 1965.

Hurst took the gamble. He agreed to furnish a special transmission shifter and forged aluminum wheels, and he told Bill Summers to quit his job so that both brothers could concentrate on building "Goldenrod." He said that if other sponsorship failed to materialize, he would carry the entire financial load himself. With George Hurst's endorsement, however, three additional primary sponsors were quickly brought into the project——Chrysler Corporation, Firestone Tire and Rubber Company and Mobil Oil.

Bobby designed and engineered the car, utitiliz-

George Hurst (left) and Bob Summers look over a wind tunnel model of the "Goldenrod." *Courtesy Chrysler Motor Company.*

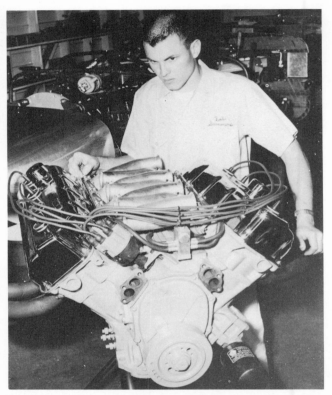

Bob Summers examines one of the four Chrysler Hemi engines that powers "Goldenrod." *Courtesy Chrysler Motor Company.*

Bob Summers and Bob Martin check a sketch of the "Goldenrod." *Courtesy Firestone Tire & Rubber Company.*

ing a unique drive system. He arranged the Chrysler V-8 hemi-engines in pairs, the front two driving the front wheels and the rear pair operating the rear wheels. A common driveline along the left side of the car kept all four engines turning at the same speed. Except for dry sump, lubrication and fuel injection—required for low overall height——the engines were stock specifications throughout. The 426 cubic inch powerplants generated a combined 2400 horsepower.

Bob Summers examines one of the differential units for "Goldenrod." *Courtesy Chrysler Motor Company.*

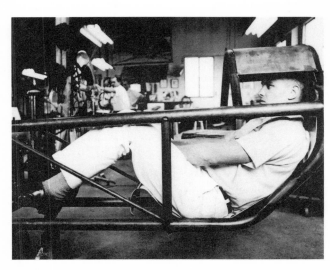

Bob Summers assumes his semi-reclining driving position in the chassis tubes and seat of "Goldenrod." *Courtesy Chrysler Motor Company.*

"Goldenrod" without body panels. Bob Summers in cockpit. *Courtesy Chrysler Motor Company.*

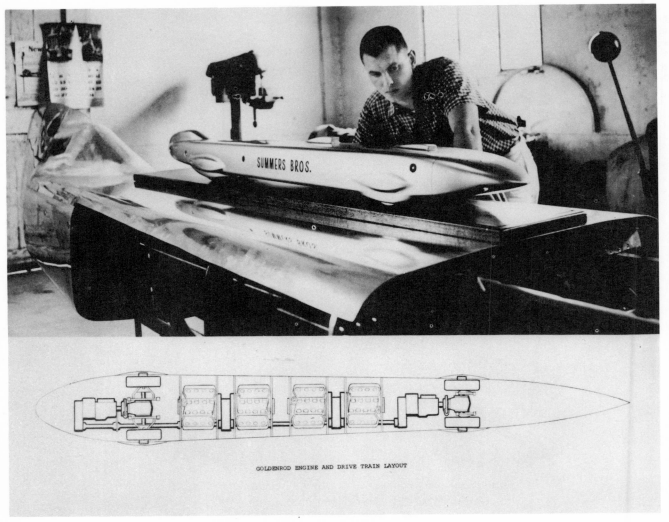

GOLDENROD ENGINE AND DRIVE TRAIN LAYOUT

Bob Summers checks scale model of "Goldenrod." *Courtesy Chrysler Motor Company.*

Firestone supplied special 600-mph nylon tubeless tires. Mobil developed special lubricants to withstand gear heat and pressure and prepared the super premium racing gasoline. Hurst developed the intricate two-unit transmission system which was placed between Summers' knees. By what engineers called a "series hook-up," he was able to shift two transmissions through an "H" pattern simultaneously with each gear change.

Lean and long, the "Goldenrod" was 32 feet overall, 48 inches wide at the front wheels and only 28 inches above the ground at the hood. The highest point was 42 inches at the tail fin. The frame was constructed of steel, the body material

of aluminum. Total weight was 5500 to 6000 pounds.

By working round-the-clock, the Summers Brothers had the "Goldenrod" ready for the wheel-driven assault in 1965.

The record didn't come easy.

In early September, a smooth practice run was made at 220 with only six miles of usable salt. Bobby really needed twice that much for maximum acceleration.

Then problems began to develop—minor fuel injection adjustments, a wiring short, a potential failure in the drive-line coupler that required redesign and a trip to Salt Lake City, a sticky shifting cable, a broken hydraulic steering line. He even made a run on three engines when someone forgot to connect a coil wire to the fourth power plant.

It seemed that each time the car was ready, the weather turned sour. One afternoon, during the first week, the wind kicked up to 40 miles an hour just before a practice run.

In mid-September, with 12 miles of usable salt, strong gusts blew water over the first four miles of the course.

But, little by little, the speed went up. During an easy 244.9 ride, Bobby pronounced that stability was good and it appeared that the bugs had been worked out.

On September 27, Summers was clocked at 373.5. It was essentially a practice run, since the car was still in third gear. In spite of the wet salt and poor traction he felt the record was attainable the next morning. However, heavy winds that night drove standing water across the track.

So the Summers Brothers dejectedly returned home with the "Goldenrod" to wait for another attempt. Back in their shop, the car was stripped, cleaned, and checked and repairs were made.

Back at the Flats in late October, the string of back luck continued after two practice runs, one at more than 400 miles an hour. After the runs, a worn wheel bearing and a damaged transfer case gear were discovered, forcing the brothers back to California to make repairs.

"Goldenrod" without body panels. *Courtesy Chrysler Motor Company.*

Bob Summers. *Courtesy Chrysler Motor Company.*

"Goldenrod." *Courtesy Chrysler Motor Company.*

"Goldenrod" in action. *Courtesy Chrysler Motor Company.*

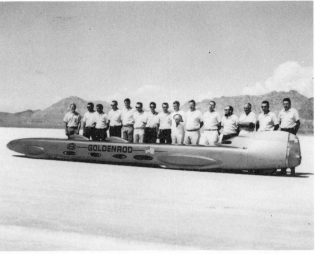

Crew of "Goldenrod." *Courtesy Chrysler Motor Company.*

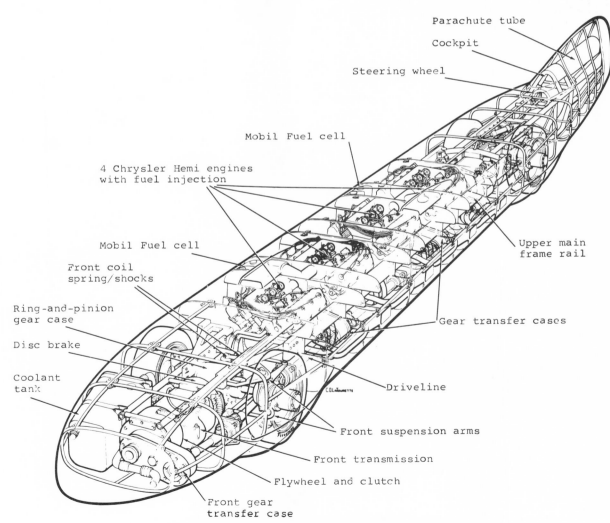

Parachute tube

Cockpit

Steering wheel

Mobil Fuel cell

4 Chrysler Hemi engines
with fuel injection

Mobil Fuel cell

Front coil
spring/shocks

Ring-and-pinion
gear case

Disc brake

Coolant
tank

Upper main
frame rail

Gear transfer cases

Driveline

Front suspension arms

Front transmission

Flywheel and clutch

Front gear
transfer case

Sketch of interior of "Goldenrod." *Courtesy Firestone Tire
& Rubber Company.*

159

Yet on that day—October 25—Bobby Summers proved that his four-engine creation had the capability of bringing back the wheel-driven mark to America after an absence of 37 years. His two-way average through the measured mile was 383.959, including a 405.095 clocking through the kilo.

Seventeen days later all systems were go.

Summers roared through the flying mile at 412.702 and 409.243 in the kilo during his north-to-south run. Fifty-five minutes later, "Golden-rod" was refueled and the parachutes repacked. Bobby Summers was securely strapped into the cockpit.

While his south-to-north return run (405.908) was almost five miles an hour slower than his first burst, it was still fast enough to assure Summers the world land speed record for wheel-driven automobiles.

An hour later it started raining—and kept on raining.

18
Magnificent Mickey

Mickey Thompson should be satisfied.

He's set 485 international and national speed records. He's one of the big names in drag racing, with his stable of high-speed "horses" performing all over the country. He's been an innovator in Indianapolis. Al Miller drove one of his light weight creations to a ninth-place finish in 1963.

In 1969, the California Senate honored its native son for "bringing considerable glory to his state and country" and for "having the skill and promotional ability to develop a small speed performance business into a million-dollar corporation."

Mickey Thompson has fame. He has wealth. Yet the one thing he wants has eluded him for more than a decade. He wants the land speed record for wheel-driven cars.

"My goal is to hit 425 miles an hour on the Flats, then I'll quit."

It's a strange goal, considering rocket and jet-propelled missiles are shooting for the sound barrier.

He knows he has the car to shatter Bobby Summer's two-way mark of 409, set in 1965. However, Mickey is missing the financial backing, since Ford pulled out of the auto-racing business.

It takes big money to run for the land speed record. Just ask Collene Campbell, Mickey's sister and publicity director: "Without a sponsor it is extremely difficult for an individual to shoulder this financial burden. As it stands right now, due to the lack of sponsorship by the big automobile companies, Mickey does not plan to drive the car in the foreseeable future."

Thompson's potential record-breaker was built

in 1968. The "Autolite Special," a twin-engine streamliner powered by a pair of Ford engines boasting 2,000 horsepower, made its land speed debut that fall. On October 30, the 30-foot car skidded out of control at speeds exceeding 400 miles an hour. Mickey was clocked at 303 in a two-mile stretch and was still accelerating when he went into a slide. During one point he was heading straight for the United States Auto Club's timing shack, but managed to steer the 5400-pound runaway away from the building. He missed the building by 75 yards.

Mickey estimates he would have driven the "Autolite Special" through the timing traps at 435 miles an hour had he remained on course.

Undaunted by his failure to set the record, Thompson returned in 1969. "We ran the car on two occasions that year," he recalls, "attaining 360 the first week. The instrumentation inside the car checked out exactly with the official clocking speed."

Mickey returned home to check the car over. A few weeks later he was back at Bonneville "to go all out. After a few dry runs we were ready. But the water season was closing in fast and the strip would be under water for seven months.

"The morning of our attempt it rained on three sections of the course for about three miles. However, I made a run which was recorded at 411 in a one-way direction.

"Due to the wet salt the car went out of control and off the course for about one mile. Consequently we missed the last timing light and were not officially timed for the run."

Mickey was willing to wait around for a break in

Mickey Thompson. *Courtesy Ford Motor Company.*

brakes on all four wheels and three rear-opening parachutes. Basic dimensions for the car: overall length, 29 feet, 7 inches; height at nose, 27 inches, and at canopy, 37 inches; width, 34-7/8 inches, and weight, 5400 pounds.

Mickey's fascination with the Bonneville Salt Flats dates back to 1937. His boyhood hero was Frank Lockhart, who was killed during a land-speed attempt at Ormond Beach, Florida. Lockhart was only 24.

He was born Marion Lee Thompson, Jr., on December 7, 1928, in San Fernando, California. By the time he was 12, he had assembled a coaster that ran uphill on junk storage batteries he picked up for 12 cents apiece. Two years later Mickey found a '27 Chevy coupe. He paid $7.50 for the junker, put it together from bits and pieces and later resold the same car for $125.

Later, he bought a model A roadster for $9. It was his first hot rod. Before he was old enough for a driver's license, Thompson gunned the heap to a speed of 79 at El Mirage Dry Lake. His patched-up job had farm implement tires in front that were guaranteed to be safe at 5 miles an hour.

the weather. He didn't want to leave the Flats, not when he was so close.

"Ford Motor Company then chose to have us run the funny cars on the drag racing circuit. That kept us so busy that time did not permit us to go back to Bonneville for the land-speed record."

Aerodynamically, experts at Ford said the car had a speed capacity of 500 miles an hour.

The aerodynamic concepts were determined during a series of wind-tunnel tests on a one-fourth scale model. The design called for the driver to be positioned between the two 427 cubic inch single overhead-cam engines. A supercharged version in the rear produces 1260 horsepower for the back wheels, while the front engine supplies 810 horsepower to the front wheels. Thompson drove reclined between the two powerplants.

The chassis is of space-frame construction, using square and round tubular steel. It is cross-beamed. The shell is lightweight aluminum. Braking is accomplished with the aid of ventilated disc

Mickey Thompson in "Challenger I."

"Challenger I," powered by four supercharged Pontiac engines, turned an officially timed one-way speed of 406.6 mph. *Courtesy Goodyear Tire & Rubber Company.*

Mickey Thompson and "Challenger I." *Courtesy Goodyear Tire and Rubber Company.*

"Challenger I." *Courtesy Goodyear Tire & Rubber Company.*

"Challenger I" and crew.

To support his "habit," Mickey mowed lawns, sold papers and worked on other people's cars. Mechanics came easy to him.

By 1949 he was hitting 90 miles an hour at the Santa Ana drag strip. Three years later he gunned

The fruits of victory.

his tandem-engine hot rod to a national speed record of 194.34.

Never satisfied, Thompson sought other challenges. In 1954 and 1955 he entered the grueling Pan Am, a 1900-mile test of man and machine across Mexico. Both races ended in crashes.

He also tried his hand at closed-circuit sports car driving. A 1957 crash at treacherous Riverside in California resulted in a broken kneecap.

During those hectic years Mickey made $350 to $400 a week, but he did it the hard way. He worked as a pressman at the Los Angeles Times, ran the Lions Club drag strip in Long Beach, and also had his own garage.

All this time he was thinking of the Salt Flats and the land-speed record. As early as 1952 Mickey made sketches of a streamliner, with two engines driving the four wheels.

Six years later a few lines on a drawing pad came to life in the form of a snarling, twin-engine slingshot dragster.

Mickey's target was the 266.2 clocking, set by

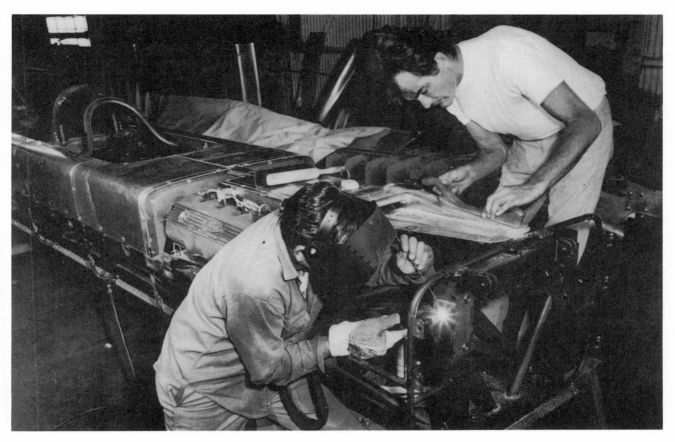

Workmen in Mickey Thompson's Long Beach, Calif., shop assemble the chassis for the "Ford-Autolite Special."

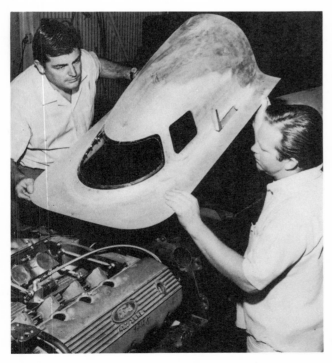

Mickey Thompson (left) and Pat Foster fit the aluminum canopy into place on "Autolite." In the foreground is one of the four 427-cubic-inch Ford single overhead cam engines that powers the car. *Courtesy Ford Motor Company.*

Mickey Thompson and "Autolite Special," waiting for good weather to begin their run. *Courtesy Ford Motor Company.*

Micky Thompson and the "Autolite Special."

Bill Kenz in 1957. Kenz' reign as the fastest American on wheels was about to come to an end. Using gas as a propellent, Thompson hit an easy 159 in a mile run that lasted 9.72 seconds. Methodically he increased the speed to 241...251. Then Mickey bettered Kenz's effort with a two-way 266.866 average.

But that wasn't fast enough.

Adding 30 per cent nitro, Thompson startled American speed enthusiasts by driving his 800-horsepower creation to a speed of 290 miles an hour.

He was getting close to his goal.

Since 1927, the world's land-speed record had been broken 15 times, all on American soil—first at Ormond Beach and then at Bonneville.

But during that time only one American had held the record. That was in 1928 when Ray Keech hit 207.55 in the three-engine "Triplex." His record stood for only one year.

Mickey was shooting at the late John Cobb's record of 394.20, set in 1947. England ruled the world of speed.

He called his car "Challenger I." It was small by land-speed standards, being eight feet shorter and three feet narrower than Cobb's 6,700-pound "Railton Special." Mickey's hot rod weighed less than 5,000 pounds. Powered by four 450 horse-

Mickey Thompson (left)promoted his first long course off-road race. It had 240 entries in February, 1974. *Courtesy Mickey Thompson/Rapid Pace.*

166

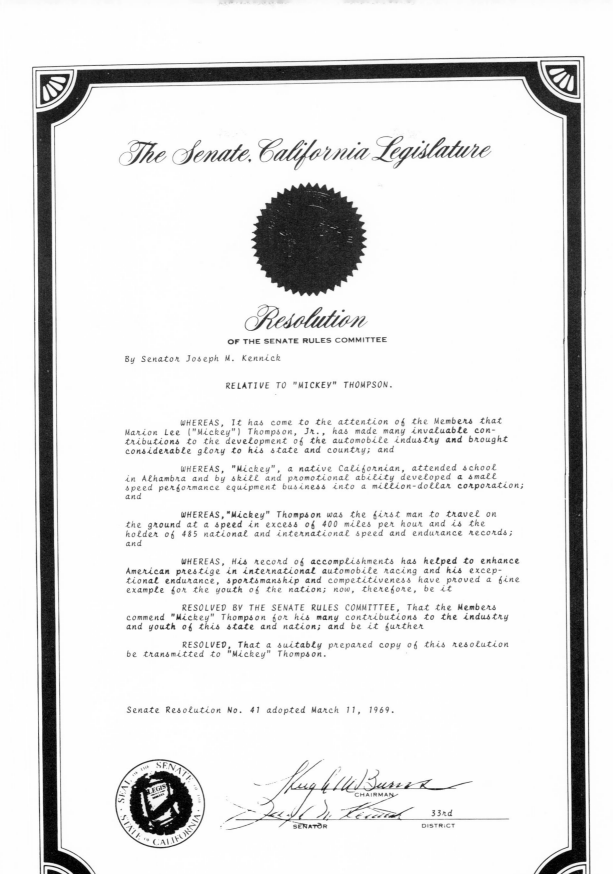

The Senate, California Legislature

Resolution

OF THE SENATE RULES COMMITTEE

By Senator Joseph M. Kennick

RELATIVE TO "MICKEY" THOMPSON.

WHEREAS, It has come to the attention of the Members that Marion Lee ("Mickey") Thompson, Jr., has made many invaluable contributions to the development of the automobile industry and brought considerable glory to his state and country; and

WHEREAS, "Mickey", a native Californian, attended school in Alhambra and by skill and promotional ability developed a small speed performance equipment business into a million-dollar corporation; and

WHEREAS, "Mickey" Thompson was the first man to travel on the ground at a speed in excess of 400 miles per hour and is the holder of 485 national and international speed and endurance records; and

WHEREAS, His record of accomplishments has helped to enhance American prestige in international automobile racing and his exceptional endurance, sportsmanship and competitiveness have proved a fine example for the youth of the nation; now, therefore, be it

RESOLVED BY THE SENATE RULES COMMITTEE, That the Members commend "Mickey" Thompson for his many contributions to the industry and youth of this state and nation; and be it further

RESOLVED, That a suitably prepared copy of this resolution be transmitted to "Mickey" Thompson.

Senate Resolution No. 41 adopted March 11, 1969.

CHAIRMAN

SENATOR   33rd

DISTRICT

The State of California honored native son Mickey Thompson in 1969. *Courtesy Mickey Thompson/Rapid Pace.*

power Pontiac engines, "Challenger I" was publically unveiled in August of 1959. Mickey made no boasts that day. He didn't promise any miracles.

"I don't promise to break the land-speed record. No one can make such a promise. But I think I can promise you that I will go faster than any American ever had; that means breaking my own

Dr. Nathan Ostich and Great Britain's Donald Campbell came to Bonneville with jets. Art Arfons and Athol Graham relied on piston power from the brutish V-12 Allison aircraft engine.

Thompson added four blowers to increase his horsepower. He also brought along JATO rockets for additional thrust. However, the governing

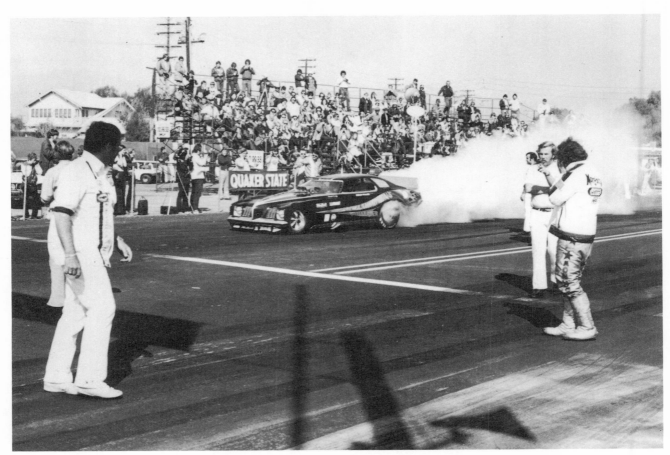

Mickey Thompson's '74 dragster blasts off the starting line.
Courtesy Mickey Thompson/Rapid Pace.

record. And I'll do it with equipment down to the last cotter pin."

Mickey kept his word, hitting a top average of 330.51 miles per hour. Before rain prevented any more record attempts, Thompson powered "Challenger I" to a new American flying mile record of 363.67.

While Mickey was stealing the headlines, a group of challengers were preparing for a 1960 showdown.

bodies of auto racing ruled the rockets illegal.

One by one the challengers failed. Graham's record bid ended in tragedy when the tail section fell off his car which leaped in the air and crashed. Graham died two hours later.

Campbell's massive "Bluebird" did a 360 mph slide. Campbell escaped with a concussion.

For three weeks everything had gone wrong for Mickey Thompson. Then things began looking up. On September 4, he clocked an effortless 372.67.

When a driveshaft broke three days later, Mickey should have realized it was an omen of things to come.

On September 9, Thompson and "Challenger I"

Mickey Thompson streaks along, testing the 7½ mile course he prepared for easy viewing by spectators and rough riding for racers at the Mickey Thompson-Delco R V Spectacular at Riverside Raceway. *Courtesy Mickey Thompson/Rapid Pace.*

roared across the Flats at 406.60. It marked the first time an American had cracked the 400 barrier. It was a good run from the start. At the end of the track, mechanics swarmed all over the home-made car. The streamliner looked perfect. Mickey walked around making personal checks and shaking hands with reporters. His hands were steady.

"I'm not nervous, look at that," he commented. "I never felt better."

Within minutes the "Challenger" began its return run to cement the record. But it soon became obvious that the car was in trouble as it just coasted into the timing zone.

Mickey had come so close, only to be stymied by a driveshaft that snapped when he shifted into second gear at about 210 miles an hour.

Dejectedly he vowed, "We'll be back in a week. I guess we just stressed everything in the car. The whole crew needs a rest and I want to see my kids again."

It was "Challenger's" last hurrah.

Despite the failure, Mickey is convinced the car never reached its speed potential. "This car would have run considerably faster if we had not been continually plagued with drive gear problem—and taking into consideration the particular design of the car, it was almost impossible to patch."

Thompson planned to return to the Flats with "Challenger." That was before he broke his back driving a twin-engine dragster across Lake Meade, Nevada.

"I was told that I would never drive again and the car was put aside with no further work being done. It was then that I decided to concentrate on making money for the next few years."

But Mickey did drive again. On July 9, 1961, he invaded March Air Force base in Riverside, California and piloted four different cars to 14 international and national speed records during a five-hour marathon.

He started racing just after dawn and didn't quit until 25-mile-an-hour gusts stopped him short during final runs at 11:30 a.m. Thompson waited another hour for the wind to die before he canceled a schedule which would raised a new record total to 18.

Why risk $75,000 worth of racing equipment in setting the marks?

His efforts, he said, "were partly for my own satisfaction and partly for the world prestige of my country."

Mickey Thompson's 1973 Pontiac Grand Am dragster. *Courtesy Mickey Thompson/Rapid Pace.*

Fastest time was just over 240 aboard a modified Class C special, "Assault I."

Even when the land speed emphasis shifted

from piston to jets and rockets, Mickey held firm. Maybe he's just too stubborn to give up a boyhood dream.

"I've built and driven a jet to a new strip record the first time out. I find it takes no skill to drive the car and really no mechanical knowledge to make it go fast."

No doubt if Mickey wanted to travel 800 miles an hour, he would build a missile on wheels. But he's not interested in speed for speed's sake.

Mickey Thompson grew up in the era when men pushed automobiles across the sands of Ormond Beach. His boyhood hero was Frank Lockhart, who was killed on that Florida raceway.

He's a "purist" who believes in piston power. So 425 miles an hour is fine with him.

19
Beginning ... or the End?

Man has been faced by a series of barriers for countless years. History is filled with such instances. Columbus, for instance, lived in a time when men thought the earth was flat—that he and his small fleet would tumble into an abyss once they reached the edge.

The Wright Brothers proved that man could fly. Another barrier had been broken.

Likewise, speed barriers have been placed in front of man ever since he learned to harness the powers of electricity, steam and later internal combustion, jet and rocket engines.

Count de Chasseloup-Laubat, a Frenchman, started the great chase in 1898 when he drove his electric car through the mile in 57 seconds. His speed: 39.34 miles an hour.

Six years later another Frenchman, Louis Rigolly, became the first to shatter the 100 mile an hour barrier. He went 103:55.

Until Henry Segrave of England crashed the 200 mph barrier, experts said a car would break up at that speed—that the wheels would fly off, or the cars would take off and fly. Seagrave proved otherwise by becoming the first to travel three miles a minute.

One by one, the barriers came tumbling down.08

Sir Malcolm Campbell went 301 mph in 1935...Craig Breedlove 407 in 1963...Craig Breedlove 526 in 1964...Craig Breedlove 600.601. in 1965.

Five years later, Gary Gabelich of Long Beach, California drove his rocket car to a land speed record of 622.407 mph.

But who will break the 700 mph Barrier? Has man reached a barrier that is finally too formidable to penetrate?

Experts are divided as to whether man can travel faster than sound on land. That means 720-750 miles an hour, depending on such factors as altitude, air density and temperature.

Some feel there is no reason why such a feat cannot be accomplished. Others call the undertaking "too dangerous."

Again the phraseology of yesteryear is repeated—that a car would break up at that speed, or take off and fly.

The drivers all agree. "It's a gamble," they say. But they're all willing to take a chance in this high-stakes game.

No doubt the first driver through the sound barrier will have it made, financially. But it takes more than money to put a man in the cockpit.

Craig Breedlove says it best. "Let's face it. When you sit down in that cockpit, all the money in the world isn't going to make you drive that car if you don't really want the record."

Certainly three-time world land speed king Art Arfons doesn't do it primarily for the money. "Financially, I haven't made money out of land speed racing. So why do I do it? I don't know how to explain it. It's really something I don't understand myself. Maybe because it's there."

Not even the possibility of death deters these modern-day explorers from taking a step into the unknown.

Says Gary Gabelich:

"If I should die because of my racing, at least my parents and close friends will know I went out with a smile on my face. I think of myself as a lion tamer. With all that horsepower, you try to utilize as much of it as possible without getting hurt. There's a fine line between control of the car and complete disaster. That's what makes it so challenging.''

Some may die in this supersonic quest, but man will travel faster than sound. The horsepower is there. So is the knowledge.

And once the last "barrier" is broken, that will bring the end of what has been known as land speed racing. From then on it will just be a matter of going faster.

Gabelich envisions that man may be running on "light rays, laser beams, or something like that.''

He's probably right.

The ulitmate speed limit will be determined by the length of the racetrack.

Back in 1935 when Campbell became the first to crack the 300 miles an hour barrier with his two-way clocking of 301.13 at the Bonneville Salt Flats, a reporter on the scene asked the gutsy Englishman if he had reached the ultimate speed.

To which Campbell answered:

"No I have not set a record I cannot beat. I can build a car that will go much faster, and I shall probably do that. Nor have I set a record that another driver can't beat. No man could do that, for what I can do another man can do.''

Bibliography

Campbell, Sir Malcolm. *Speed on Wheels*. London. Sampson Low, Marston & Co., Ltd. 1949.

Clifton, Paul. *The Fastest Men on Earth*. London. Herbert Jenkins Ltd., 1964.

Jenkins, Abe and Ashton, Wendell, J. The Salt of the Earth. Los Angeles. Clymer Motors. 1945.

Katz, Frederic. *Art Arfons: Fastest Man On Wheels*. London, New York, Toronto. Rutledge. 1965.

Pearson, John. *The Last Hero. The Gallant Story of Donald Campbell and the Land-Speed Record, 1964*. New York. David McKay Company. 1966.

Thompson, Mickey with Borgeson, Griffith. *Challenger. Mickey Thompson's Own Story of His Life of Speed*. Englewood Cliffs, New Jersey. Prentice-Hall. 1964.

Villa, Leo. *The Record Breakers. Sir Malcolm and Donald Campbell, Land and Water-Speed Kings of the 20th Century*. London, New York, Sydney, Toronto. Paul Hamlyn. 1969.

Zarem, Lewis. *New Dimensions of Flight*. New York. E.P. Dutton & Co. 1959.

Index

7